PALM BEACH COUNTY
LIBRARY SYSTEM
3650 Summit Boulevard
West Palm Beach, FL 33406-4198

Life in the Sea

The Open Ocean

Pam Walker and
Elaine Wood

Facts On File, Inc.

The Open Ocean

Facts On File, Inc.
132 West 31st Street
New York NY 10001

Library of Congress Cataloging-in-Publication Data
Walker, Pam, 1958–
The open ocean / Pam Walker and Elaine Wood.
p. cm.—(Life in the sea)
Includes bibliographical references and index.
ISBN 0-8160-5705-2 (hardcover)
1. Oceanography—Juvenile literature. 2. Marine animals—Juvenile literature.
3. Marine ecology—Juvenile literature. I. Wood, Elaine. II. Title.
GC21.5.W35 2005
578.77—dc22   2004024228

Facts On File books are available at special discounts when purchased in bulk
quantities for businesses, associations, institutions, or sales promotions.
Please call our Special Sales Department in New York at
(212) 967-8800 or (800) 322-8755.

You can find Facts On File on the World Wide Web at
http://www.factsonfile.com

Text and cover design by Dorothy M. Preston
Illustrations by Dale Williams, Sholto Ainslie, and Dale Dyer

Printed in the United States of America

VB FOF 10 9 8 7 6 5 4 3 2 1

This book is printed on acid-free paper.

Contents

Preface

Life first appeared on Earth in the oceans, about 3.5 billion years ago. Today these immense bodies of water still hold the greatest diversity of living things on the planet. The sheer size and wealth of the oceans are startling. They cover two-thirds of the Earth's surface and make up the largest habitat in this solar system. This immense underwater world is a fascinating realm that captures the imaginations of people everywhere.

Even though the sea is a powerful and immense system, people love it. Nationwide, more than half of the population lives near one of the coasts, and the popularity of the seashore as a home or place of recreation continues to grow. Increasing interest in the sea environment and the singular organisms it conceals is swelling the ranks of marine aquarium hobbyists, scuba divers, and deep-sea fishermen. In schools and universities across the United States, marine science is working its way into the science curriculum as one of the foundation sciences.

The purpose of this book is to foster the natural fascination that people feel for the ocean and its living things. As a part of the set entitled Life in the Sea, this book aims to give readers a glimpse of some of the wonders of life that are hidden beneath the waves and to raise awareness of the relationships that people around the world have with the ocean.

This book also presents an opportunity to consider the ways that humans affect the oceans. At no time in the past have world citizens been so poised to impact the future of the planet. Once considered an endless and resilient resource, the ocean is now being recognized as a fragile system in danger of overuse and neglect. As knowledge and understanding about the ocean's importance grow, citizens all over the world can participate in positively changing the ways that life on land interacts with life in the sea.

Acknowledgments

$\mathcal{T}$his opportunity to study and research ocean life has reminded both of us of our past love affairs with the sea. Like many families, ours took annual summer jaunts to the beach, where we got our earliest gulps of salt water and fingered our first sand dollars. As sea-loving children, both of us grew into young women who aspired to be marine biologists, dreaming of exciting careers spent nursing wounded seals, surveying the dark abyss, or discovering previously unknown species. After years of teaching school, these dreams gave way to the reality that we did not get to spend as much time in the oceans as we had hoped. But time and distance never diminished our love and respect for it.

We are thrilled to have the chance to use our own experiences and appreciation of the sea as platforms from which to develop these books on ocean life. Our thanks go to Frank K. Darmstadt, executive editor at Facts On File, for this enjoyable opportunity. He has guided us through the process with patience, which we greatly appreciate. Frank's skills are responsible for the book's tone and focus. Our appreciation also goes to Katy Barnhart for her copyediting expertise.

Special notes of appreciation go to several individuals whose expertise made this book possible. Audrey McGhee proofread and corrected pages at all times of the day or night. Diane Kit Moser, Ray Spangenburg, and Bobbi McCutcheon, successful and seasoned authors, mentored us on techniques for finding appropriate photographs. We appreciate the help of these generous and talented people.

Introduction

$\mathcal{T}$ he largest portion of Earth, the oceanic realm, is made up of the deep seas and the open oceans. The size of this region is staggering. The volume of the oceanic world is 170 times larger than all of the terrestrial habitats plus the habitats of the upper layer of the oceans. Because of its formidable size and harsh conditions, this vast region has been explored less than any other part of our planet. As a result, it is the subject of much current research in marine biology and oceanography.

The Open Ocean is one title in Life in the Sea, a six-volume set that will share both the wonders and the science of marine ecosystems. *The Open Ocean* provides the reader with a picture of life in those farthest regions of the sea, well past the shallow coastal zones and familiar continental shelves.

Chapter 1 examines the features of the ocean floor as well as the vertical zones of the ocean, each zone defined by depth. The three-dimensional aspect of the oceanic world makes life there very different from life on the land. Chapter 1 sets the stage for understanding sea life in the open and deep ocean by introducing critical physical parameters like salinity, temperature, depth, light, and density. Particular attention is paid to the unique characteristics of deep-sea environments of hydrothermal vents and cold-water coral reefs.

In chapter 2, *The Open Ocean* examines the one-celled organisms that form the base of ocean food chains. Microscopic green organisms that live in the topmost layer of seawater use the Sun's energy to produce enough food to support almost every living thing in the sea. On a much smaller scale, newly discovered microbes on the deep seafloor live without the Sun's energy, generating the energy needed for life from chemical reactions. Plants are conspicuously absent from the open-ocean environment, lacking a place of attachment and enough light and nutrients to survive. The exception is the brown alga sargassum weed, a plant that forms miles of floating rafts in the Atlantic Ocean. Chapter 2 also emphasizes the contributions of decomposers, organisms that break down large molecules, explaining how they support the marine food chain.

Chapters 3 and 4 examine some of the deep and open ocean invertebrates, animals without backbones. Without a doubt, many of these creatures are unusual in comparison to the organisms found in shallow waters. The habitats of invertebrates vary tremendously with depth. Sponges and cnidarians are responsible for building two types of deepwater habitats, the glass-sponge reefs and the cold-water coral reefs. Compared to the rest of the seafloor, these habitats are busy metropolises of deepwater life. Reefs of all types provide places for animals to hide, mate, lay eggs, and hunt, making them valuable environments. Worms are one of the largest constituents of any marine environment, including the reefs. On the hydrothermal vents, worms reach gargantuan sizes, measuring up to four feet (1.2 m) long.

Mollusks are common on both the seafloor and at the top of the water column, where they exist in unusual forms such as the delicate sea butterflies. Clams, mussels, octopuses, and squid are mollusks that can be found in areas of the deep ocean where food is available. One group of echinoderms, the sea cucumbers, are more numerous on deep seafloors than in any other part of the ocean. Arthropods, such as crabs and shrimp, are found at hydrothermal vents, deepwater reefs, and glass-sponge reefs.

Fish, the topic of chapter 5, are the largest group of vertebrates, or animals that have backbones. The habitats of fish are largely defined by depth and physical factors such as temperature and oxygen. Fish that live in the upper levels of the sea include flying fish (animals that can soar in the air for long distances on elongated pectoral fins), as well as wahoo, mackerel, sailfish, tiger sharks, whitetip sharks, basking sharks, and pelagic stingrays. In the middle zone of water, fish show some remarkable adaptations that help them survive in an environment where light and food are sparse. Lanternfish and viperfish are two species that generate their own light through the process of bioluminescence. Viperfish, hatchetfish, and dragonfish are a few of the many fish that have elongated, sharp teeth, an adaptation that assures them success in catching prey. Fish that live near the bottom of the deep sea show adaptations to high pressure, cold temperature, and lack of food. Although the seafloor is the home to a wide variety of fish, the populations of each kind are slim. Gulper eels and anglerfish are two of several species that have enormous mouths, enabling them to catch and consume prey larger than their own bodies. With so little food around, deepwater fish cannot afford to miss any opportunity to feed.

Open-ocean reptiles, birds, and mammals are discussed in chapter 6. Though smaller in number than fish, these vertebrates are highly visible and play important roles at the top of open-sea food chains. The reptiles are the smallest group, made up of the yellow-bellied sea snake and a few species of marine turtles. Birds that live in the open-ocean zone spend most of their time at sea, but travel to shore to breed and raise their young. Most open-ocean birds produce only one chick a year simply because their sources of food, the fish and invertebrates of the open ocean, are too far from terrestrial nesting sites to feed larger broods. Mammals in the open and deep sea include only a few species of seals and dolphins, but a large number of whales. Many species of whales travel extensively, dividing their time between the northern and southern hemispheres.

Chapter 7 examines both the past and the future of deep-sea research. Only 150 years ago, this region was considered to be uninhabitable. Human understanding of the deep sea has improved dramatically. In just the last 30 years, the number and diversity of organisms brought from the deep sea have shocked and thrilled scientists. Based on what they have learned so far, plans are in the works for ongoing studies in the largest, and least understood, part of the Earth's environment.

In an age when people have so much knowledge at their fingertips, the unknown wonders of the deep generate a welcome sense of excitement and awe. *The Open Ocean* starts the reader on an adventure into an awe-inspiring seascape fill with exotic creatures. Perhaps this glimpse of the mysterious, deepwater world will inspire a new generation of marine scientists to even greater discoveries.

Physical Aspects
Light, Depth, and Chemistry of the Open Ocean

The majority of the sea, the portion referred to as the deep, open ocean, lies beyond the relatively shallow waters of the continental shelves. Covering more than 50 percent of the Earth's surface, this watery universe is the planet's largest habitat. No one knows for sure how many organisms live in the open sea, but scientists estimate that between 500,000 and 100 million different kinds of living things make their homes there.

Less is known about the deep and open portions of the ocean than of any other area of the planet. The very magnitude of these waters has made them as difficult to study as outer space. Waters in this unknown frontier are so deep that the technology to explore them has only been developed in the last 40 years. Instruments like deep-sea cameras, deep-manned submersibles, and remotely operated robots have made it possible to take a look into the abyss.

Even though the surface of the open sea looks like a uniform plain of water, nothing could be further from the truth. The open ocean is a complex system that is influenced by geological, chemical, physical, and biological factors. A scientist surveying 1,000 different locations in the ocean would find that each is unique. By the same token, the number and types of living things vary by location.

Profile of the Ocean Floor

Although the average ocean depth is 12,179 feet (3,700 m), the deep ocean includes waters ranging from 656 feet (200 m) to 36,213.9 feet (11,038 m). As shown in Figure 1.1, the profile of the deep ocean floor begins where the edges of the continents drop off sharply in depth. The incline of this steep

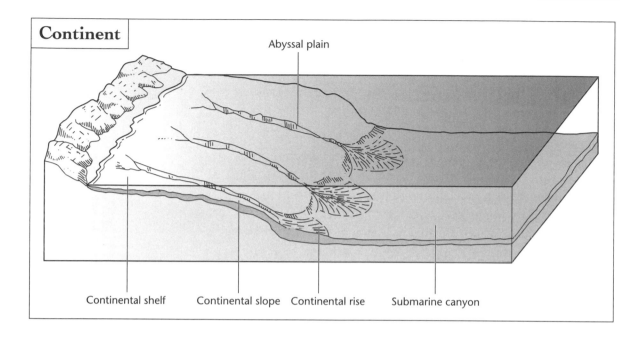

Continent

Abyssal plain

Continental shelf   Continental slope   Continental rise   Submarine canyon

Fig. 1.1   The continental shelf begins a downward slant at the continental slope. At the foot of the slope is the continental rise. Submarine canyons can be found in some continental slopes. Extending seaward from the continental rise is the abyssal plain.

slope at the edge of a continental shelf varies from a gentle hill to a straight drop-off, depending on the geology of the region. In some places, continental slopes contain canyons that are similar to those on land. Scientists believe that most of these canyons were formed through erosion by river water that flowed over them during periods of the Earth's history when sea levels were much lower. A few of the canyons are attributed to turbidity currents, undersea avalanches of water and sediment that move swiftly over the submerged slopes, eroding them. Turbidity currents on the continental slopes can be triggered by earthquakes or by accumulations of sediment that slide from the tops to the bases of the slopes.

At the bottom of the continental slope is the continental rise, a gentle incline composed of accumulations of sediment. The Atlantic Ocean contains more continental rises than the Pacific Ocean because, in the latter, there are many deep trenches at the base of slopes. Continental rises are also found around Antarctica and in the Indian Ocean. Beyond the continental rise is the abyssal plain, an expanse of seafloor at depths of 14,963.8 feet (4,500 m) to 16,404 feet (5,000 m). Abyssal hills frequently interrupt the flat profile of the plain, some with elevations as tall as 3,300 feet (1,000 m). Formed by undersea volcanic activity and deep earth movements, abyssal hills cover 50 percent of the Atlantic Ocean floor and 80 percent of the bottom of the Pacific Ocean.

Encircling the globe is a belt of submerged volcanic mountains called the mid-ocean ridge. Created by eons of underwater volcanic eruptions, the mid-oceanic ridge is still an active volcanic area where hot lava bubbles up to the seafloor. When lava reaches the surface, it spreads out and cools, forming a new crust on either side of the ridge. This geologic activity is the cause of a phenomenon known as seafloor spreading, the movement of the crust laterally out from the ridge and toward the continents. The creation of new crust separates pieces of the existing crust at a rate of about five inches (2 cm) a year. As the seafloor expands, the leading edge of existing crust is eventually pushed down into the magma, molten rock inside the Earth, in regions called subduction zones. In the magma, the old crust is liquefied and its components are recycled. Many subduction zones are located in deep-sea trenches, which are more common in the Pacific than Atlantic Ocean.

The most cavernous subduction zone is the Mariana Trench, located in the Pacific Ocean north of New Guinea. Within the Mariana, the deepest point is named the Challenger Deep, a spot that is 36,000 feet (about 11,000 m), or 6.8 miles (11 km), below the water. To put this depth in perspective, Mount Everest, the highest elevation on the continents, stands 29,025.6 feet (8,847 m) above sea level. Other low points include the Peru-Chile Trench, which runs along the entire west coast of South America, the Japan-Kuril Trench near Japan, and the Aleutian Trench off the Aleutian Islands in the Pacific Ocean. In the Atlantic Ocean, there are two, relatively short trenches: the South Sandwich Trench, below the southernmost tip of South America, and the Puerto Rico–Cayman Trench, between the southeastern United States and northeastern South America.

Dividing Waters

To help define marine environments, scientists divide the water column and the ocean floor into zones. Even though these zones lack sharp boundaries, they aid in the study of the ocean and its inhabitants. Each zone displays unique chemical, physical, and biological characteristics.

Two broad areas of surface water are the neritic zone and the oceanic zone. Waters over the continental shelves are described as neritic, and those above the open ocean are oceanic. In both sectors, waters are divided into sections by depth, and their assigned names are based on Greek terms. Marine scientists refer to the entire water column (as opposed to the seafloor) as pelagic, from the Greek word *pelagos,* which means "sea." The prefix *epi* is used in reference to the uppermost part of the water column. *Meso* is a prefix that means "middle," and *bathy* translates to "deep." The Greek word for very deep is *abyssal,* and the term *hadal* means "deepest," or "near Hades."

Figure 1.2 illustrates the different depth zones of the water column. The epipelagic zone, between the surface and 656.2 feet (200 m), is the topmost layer of the open ocean. Below that is the mesopelagic zone, extending down to 3,280.8 feet (1,000 m). Immediately underneath the mesopelagic zone is the bathypelagic zone, which reaches to 13,123.4 feet (4,000 m). The deepest waters are divided into the abyssopelagic zone, which includes waters as deep as 19,685 feet (6,000 m), and all of the water below is called the hadopelagic zone.

Different areas of the seafloor, or benthos, are also designated by depth. The portion that remains above the highest tides is the supralittoral zone. The intertidal, or littoral, zone is the region alternately covered and uncovered by tidal waters. Extending from the lowest tide to the edges of the continental shelf is the sublittoral, or shelf, zone. The bathyal zone includes continental slopes, rises, and the sides of mid-oceanic ridges. The abyssal zone is the region of the bottom from depths of 13,123.4 feet (4,000 m) to 19,685 feet (6,000 m), and the hadal zone is the bottom that extends below 19,685 feet (6,000 m). The seafloor itself is described as the benthic zone, and living things found on the bottom are benthos.

Fig. 1.2   The water column can be divided into regions by depth. The epipelagic zone receives enough light for photosynthesis. Only diffuse light reaches the mesopelagic or twilight zone. No sunlight penetrates the bathypelagic and abyssopelagic zones.

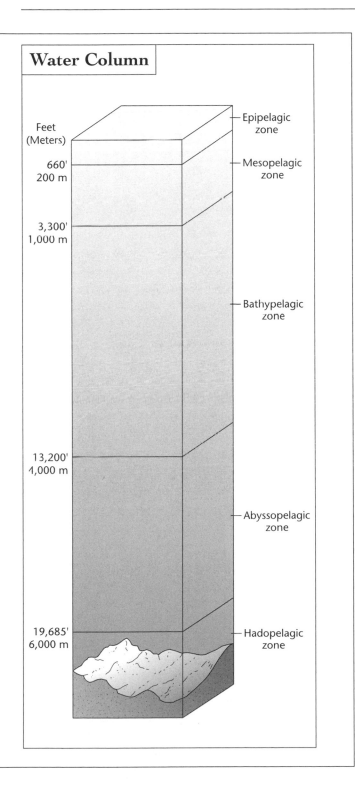

Water Column

Feet
(Meters)

660'
200 m

3,300'
1,000 m

13,200'
4,000 m

19,685'
6,000 m

Epipelagic
zone

Mesopelagic
zone

Bathypelagic
zone

Abyssopelagic
zone

Hadopelagic
zone

Water Science

As in the rest of the ocean, waters of the deep sea are defined by a set of chemical and physical characteristics that include salinity, temperature, density, light, dissolved gases, levels of nutrients, and pressure. Differences in physical traits from one region of the ocean to the next can limit the movement of sea organisms as effectively as walls or fences restrict the movements of terrestrial animals. Unlike the majority of coastal marine organisms, quite a few open ocean animals cannot tolerate varying conditions and must stay in areas that fall within limited chemical and physical parameters.

The term *salinity* refers to the concentration of dissolved minerals, or salts, in the water. In ancient times, philosophers believed that the ocean's salts originated from a salt fountain on the deep seafloor. Today, scientists know that these minerals are derived from the weathering of terrestrial materials such as limestone, granite, and shale. The erosion and transport of salts in ocean waters is an extremely slow process that has been occurring for millions of years. A small percentage of minerals also enter seawater from gases that escape from underwater volcanic vents. The primary salts in the water are sodium (31 percent) and chloride (55 percent), the components of table salt. Ocean water also contains other minerals, including calcium, magnesium, potassium, bicarbonate, sulfate, and bromide.

The average salinity of ocean water is 35 parts per thousand, meaning that for every 1,000 parts of water, there are 35 parts of minerals. In the deep parts of the ocean, salinity remains fairly constant, but in surface waters it can vary drastically. Any change that adds freshwater to the ocean decreases its salinity, so salinity is lower in surface waters in regions where there are frequent rains, such as the temperate zones. In the spring, polar surface waters experience low salinity when icebergs begin to melt.

The salinity of the ocean increases if water is removed from the system by evaporation or ice formation. When water freezes, salt is initially held in pockets within the ice structure but quickly leeches out of the forming ice into the water beneath it. For this reason, surface ocean waters in cold, ice-forming latitudes are saltier than waters in warm latitudes. The faster ice forms, the less salt can escape from it. Consequently, the saltiest seawater is found in climates where ice forms slowly. Salty water also occurs in hot, dry regions that experience high evaporation rates.

Of the world's major oceans, the North Atlantic is the saltiest, averaging a salinity of 37.9 parts per thousand. Within the North Atlantic, the section with the highest salinity is the Sargasso Sea. Located 2,000 miles (3,218.7 km) west of the Canary Islands, the Sargasso Sea is named for the floating seaweed, sargassum, which covers its surface. In this area, water is warm, 83°F (28°C), so evaporation rates are very high. In addition, the Sargasso Sea is far from land and so receives no freshwater runoff.

The temperature of seawater is a critically important characteristic to living things. Because temperature influences other characteristics of water, such as salinity, density, and concentration of dissolved gases, it can limit the distribution of organisms in the open ocean. Temperature varies by season, latitude, depth, and nearness to shore, but the average sea surface temperature (SST) of the open ocean is about

62.6°F (17°C). Because the temperature of water changes very gradually, in some parts of the ocean, especially at the equator and the poles, water temperature remains almost constant. Polar SST averages about 28.4°F (–2°C) and equatorial waters are usually about 81°F (27°C).

The temperature of ocean water is not uniform from the top to the bottom of the water column. Two distinct layers form, with a clear boundary between them. The topmost layer of water is heated by sunlight. Wind and waves mix this sun-warmed layer with water in the first 328.1 feet (100 m), keeping the entire upper area at about the same temperature. A boundary called the thermocline, a point where temperature decreases sharply with depth, develops between 328.1 feet (100 m) and 1,312.3 feet (400 m). Below the thermocline, water is much cooler, approaching 32°F (0°C). More than 90 percent of the water in the ocean lies below the thermocline.

Temperature is a significant physical factor because it affects the rate at which chemical reactions take place in both living and nonliving systems. For a chemical reaction to occur, molecules of the reactants must be in contact with one another. Molecules that are very cold move slowly and rarely, if ever, make contact. As the heat in a system increases, so does the amount of molecular motion and the likelihood that molecules will collide with one another. The higher the temperature of a system, the faster its chemical reactions take place—up to a point. Too much heat distorts the structures of molecules in living things.

Working together, salinity and temperature regulate water's density. Density is a property of matter that refers to its mass per unit volume. The higher the salinity of water, the more dissolved minerals it contains and the greater its density. Temperature influences density because it affects the volume of water. As temperature increases, water expands and takes up more space. Since the mass of warm water is spread over a larger volume than the mass of a similar amount of cool water, warm water has a lower density.

Density is the factor that determines where water will be located in the water column. Dense water sinks below less

Chemical and Physical Characteristics of Water

Water is one of the most widespread materials on this planet. Water fills the oceans, sculpts the land, and is a primary component in all living things. For all of its commonness, water is a very unusual molecule whose unique qualities are due to its physical structure.

Water is a compound made up of three atoms: two hydrogen atoms and one oxygen atom. The way these three atoms bond causes one end of the resulting molecule to have a slightly negative charge, and the other end a slightly positive charge. For this reason water is described as a polar molecule.

The positive end of one water molecule is attracted to the negative end of another water molecule. When two oppositely charged ends of water molecules get close enough to each other, a bond forms between them. This kind of bond is a hydrogen bond. Every water molecule can form hydrogen bonds with other water molecules. Even though hydrogen bonds are weaker than the bonds that hold together the atoms within a water molecule, they are strong enough to affect the nature of water and give this unusual liquid some unique characteristics.

Water is the only substance on Earth that exists in all three states of matter: solid, liquid, and gas. Because hydrogen bonds are relatively strong, a lot of energy is needed to separate water molecules from one another. That is why water can absorb more heat than any other material before its temperature increases and before it changes from one state to another.

Since water molecules stick to one another, liquid water has a lot of surface tension. Surface tension is a measure of how easy or difficult it is to break the surface of a liquid. These hydrogen bonds give water's surface a weak, membranelike quality that affects the way water forms waves and currents. The surface tension of water also impacts the organisms that live in the water column, water below the surface, as well as those on its surface.

Atmospheric gases, such as oxygen and carbon dioxide, are capable of dissolving in water, but not all gases dissolve with the same ease. Carbon dioxide dissolves more easily than oxygen, and there is always plenty of carbon dioxide in seawater. On the other hand, water holds only $\frac{1}{100}$ the volume of oxygen found in the atmosphere. Low oxygen levels in water can limit the number and types of organisms that live there. The concentration of dissolved gases is affected by temperature. Gases dissolve more easily in cold water than in warm, so cold water is richer in oxygen and carbon dioxide than warm water. Gases are also more likely to dissolve in shallow water than deep. In shallow water, oxygen gas from the atmosphere is mixed with water by winds and waves. In addition, plants, which produce oxygen gas in the process of photosynthesis, are found in shallow water.

Water Molecules

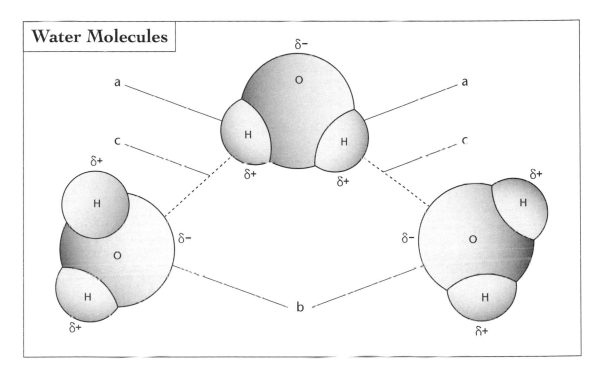

Fig. 1.3   *A water molecule is made up of two hydrogen atoms (a) bonded to one oxygen atom (b). The large nucleus of the oxygen atom causes the electrons in the resulting molecule to spend more time near the oxygen end of the molecule than near the hydrogen ends. Therefore, the oxygen end has a slightly negative charge δ⁻ and the hydrogen ends have slightly positive charges δ⁺. The slightly positive end of one water molecule is attracted to the slightly negative end of another water molecule, creating a hydrogen bond (c) between the two molecules.*

dense water, so very salty and extremely cold water is the densest kind and will always move to the lowest level of a water column. Warm seawater that is mixed with some freshwater is the least dense type, and it rides on top of the water column. Different densities of water tend to stratify, or form layers. Three conditions can increase the density of water in the upper part of the water column and cause it to stratify: cooling of the surface water by contact with cold air, formation of sea ice, and evaporation. Since stratified water does not mix easily, its layers can move past one another and retain their own characteristics. For stratified water to mix, energy must be put into the system.

Open-Ocean Light

Light, or the absence of it, is a central factor in determining which organisms can survive in marine environments. Only the upper layers of the open ocean are warmed by sunlight because warming light waves cannot penetrate deeper than 656.2 feet (200 m). The sunlit area, known as the photic zone, is the region where photosynthesis takes place. Plants and one-celled green organisms thrive in the photic zone, and they supply food for grazing animals. Just below the photic zone, at depths of 656.2 feet (200 m) to 1,640.4 feet (500 m), is the area of barely perceptible light called the twilight or dysphotic zone. The light in this region is so low that photosynthesis cannot occur and plants are unable to survive. Below the dysphotic zone is the aphotic zone, 1,640.4 feet (500 m) and deeper, where the water is completely dark. The animals that live in the dysphotic and aphotic zones either feed on food that floats down from the upper layers or travel to the upper layers to get food.

Although sunlight is plentiful in the upper layers of the open ocean, populations of photosynthetic organisms are relatively small. The factor that limits the growth and reproduction of photosynthetic organisms is not lack of light but a shortage of nutrients. Nutrient levels are lower in the open ocean than they are in any other part of the sea. Too far from land to receive steady supplies of nutrients from runoff, the barren nature of the open ocean has been likened to a desert.

Nutrients tend to become tied up in organic matter, settle out of the water column, accumulating on the seafloor well

How Light Penetrates Water

Light is a form of energy that travels in waves. When the Sun's light arrives at Earth, it has a white quality to it. White light is made up of the colors of the rainbow: violet, indigo, blue, green, yellow, orange, and red. The color of light is dependent on the length of the light wave. Light in the visible spectrum includes the colors that people can see, light whose wavelengths vary between 0.4 and 0.8 microns. (A micron is one one-millionth of a meter.) Violet light has the shortest wavelength in the visible spectrum and red has the longest.

Light is affected differently by water than it is by air. Air transmits light, but water can transmit, absorb, and reflect light, depending on its depth and contents. The fact that water transmits light makes it possible for photosynthesis to take place under water. However, all of the wavelengths of visible light do not penetrate the same depth. Blue light penetrates the most and red light the least. For that reason, if water is very clear, blue light penetrates it deeply and gives the water a blue color.

Light on the red side of the spectrum is quickly absorbed as heat, so red only penetrates to 49.2 feet (15 m). That is why water at the ocean's surface is warmer than deep water. Green light, in the middle of the spectrum, reaches greater depths; it is often reflected back from particles that are suspended in the middle range of the water column. Water that contains a lot of suspended particles, such as soil or plant matter, has a greenish brown hue.

out of the range of the one-celled green organisms that need them. At the bottom of the deep ocean, dead organic matter decomposes very slowly because temperatures are cold. In a few areas of the ocean, currents carry nutrients to the surface, but in most regions, nutrients remain trapped on the seafloor.

Ocean water and the atmosphere contain the same gases. As in the atmosphere, the major gas in ocean water is nitrogen (48 percent), followed by oxygen (36 percent), and carbon dioxide (15 percent). Oxygen is important biologically, and the presence or absence of oxygen in water is a factor that limits the kinds of organisms that can live there. The amount of oxygen that will dissolve in water is dependent on temperature and salinity. The lower the temperature and salinity of water, the easier it is for oxygen and other gases to dissolve.

Most areas of the hadal and abyssal zones, where one might expect oxygen levels to be extremely low, always contain enough oxygen to support life. Nearly all of the oxygen in the deep sea originates from surface waters in the Arctic and Antarctic regions. These cold, northern waters sink to the seafloor, supplying oxygen to the organisms that live in the lowest depths. Even though oxygen in the deepest regions of the sea is constantly consumed by animals and other organisms, it is never completely depleted.

In the upper levels of the ocean, there is always plenty of oxygen. Two sources keep the surface waters well supplied with the gas: the air and plants. Oxygen gas in the atmosphere mixes with water and dissolves in it, and plants and one-celled autotrophs living at the sea's surface produce oxygen.

A tall column of air reaches from the Earth's surface to the top of the atmosphere. The weight of this air column is referred to as air pressure. Air pressure is equal to one atmosphere (atm), or 14.7 pounds per square inch, at sea level. Water exerts far more pressure on organisms than air. Water pressure increases dramatically with depth, rising one atmosphere with each 32.8 feet (10 m). At depths of 7,500 feet (2,286 m), water exerts a pressure of 3,350 pounds on every square inch of an organism. Animals that live under so much pressure possess special adaptations in their body chemistry and structure.

Ocean Processes

Water in the ocean is constantly moving as the result of processes such as waves, wind, currents, and tides. Waves, one of the most characteristic features of the ocean, appear to be ridges of water moving across the surface. In reality, water does not travel along with a wave. Energy moves in waves through water, and the water particles simply shift up and down in small, circular paths called orbits. In most cases, the energy that sets waves in motion is the wind. Waves play an important role in mixing water in the first 328.1 feet (100 m) of the water column.

Even though water does not move from one part of the sea to another in waves, it does travel. Large masses of water pass through the seas in rivers called currents. Currents propel seawater continuously around the globe, carrying it from the surface to the deep waters and back to the surface again. Because the paths of ocean currents are long, it can take a single molecule of water about 1,000 years to make a trip around the world. Currents are generated from two sources: wind and differences in water density.

Wind-driven surface currents push about 10 percent of the oceans' waters along the same paths as the global wind belts. One of best-known surface currents is the Gulf Stream, a body of moving water that carries sun-warmed equatorial water into the northern portions of the Atlantic Ocean. Without the Gulf Stream, the range of warm-water organisms in the Atlantic Ocean would be greatly reduced and the climates of eastern North America and western Europe would be much cooler.

The movement of surface water by winds can affect the levels of nutrients in marine environments. In a few regions, including the equatorial Pacific Ocean and the west coasts of North and South America, winds blow water away from the coastline at certain times of the year. As surface water is pushed out toward the open sea, deep water flows up the water column to replace it. The arrival of nutrient-laden water to the surface supports the rapid growth of photosynthetic organisms, providing an ample food supply for fish, birds, and shellfish.

Deepwater currents do not rely on the energy of winds but are generated by differences in water densities. Since the density of seawater is largely determined by temperature and salinity, density-driven currents are also known as the thermohaline circulation, *thermo* meaning "temperature" and *haline* referring to salt. Near the poles, surface water is cooled by contact with cold, northern air, causing its density to increase. As ice forms, the salinity also increases, adding to the water's density. Eventually surface water becomes so dense that it sinks to the seafloor, displacing the water beneath it. Sinking is a very slow event, occurring at the rate of only a half inch (1.2 cm) or so a day. Water that sinks at the poles travels along the seafloors toward the equator, and then finally upwells in low and midlatitudes. Density-driven currents move a tremendous amount of water around the Earth.

Tides are the regular rising and falling of large bodies of water. Even though they are more noticeable in shallow, coastal water, tides affect the entire ocean. In deep water, movement due to tides is weaker than the movement along the coast, but the energy of underwater tides helps drive the circulation of deep-sea currents in some regions. For example, warm water that is carried to the poles by wind-driven currents cools, sinks, and travels along the seafloor toward the equator. Once the water reaches equatorial zones, the energy of deep-sea tides mixes it with less-dense water, reducing its overall density and enabling it to return to the surface.

Substrates

The ocean floor is covered in sediment that has been deposited there from several sources. Much of the material is the result of terrestrial erosion of rocks and minerals, but sediment is also supplied by animals that live in the water column, chemical reactions in the water, and particles from the atmosphere and outer space. Sediments that contain a high percentage of shells from dead marine organisms are classified as oozes. Two types of oozes are calcareous oozes, which usually form in waters less than 9,843.5 feet (3,000 m) deep, and siliceous oozes, a type often found on deeper seafloors. The presence of ooze suggests that the water above the seafloor is, or was at one time, capable of supporting living things.

Most of the material that makes up deep-sea sediments comes from the breakdown of rocks on the continents. Erosion reduces terrestrial rock to dust-sized particles that wind and water carry out to sea. The majority of this eroded material settles on the continental shelves, but some makes it to the deep ocean. The formation of sediments and oozes occurs slowly on the deep-ocean floor, accumulating at the rate of about one-half inch (1 cm) in 1,000 years. On the continental shelf, the rate of build up is faster, reaching depths of 19.7 inches (50 cm) of sediment every 1,000 years.

Much of the abyssal zone is covered with a thin layer of sediment called abyssal clay that accumulates at the extremely slow rate of a mere 0.04 inches (1 mm) every 1,000 years. An

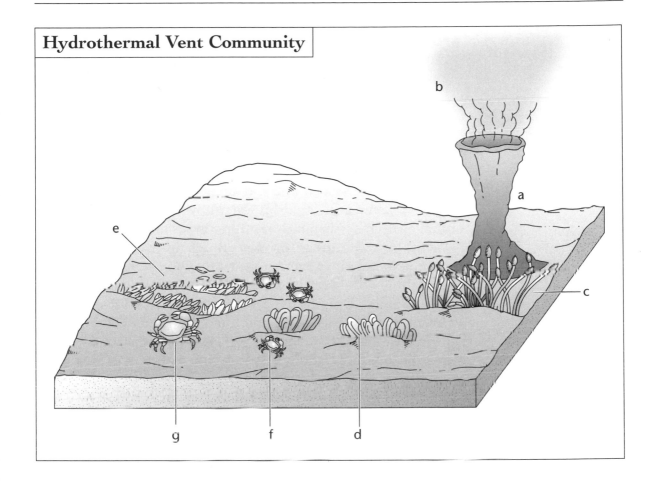

Hydrothermal Vent Community

exceptionally fine-grained material, abyssal clay forms a red or brown mud that has the texture of soft butter. The richest deposits of abyssal clay are located underneath unproductive waters, or in areas so deep that the shells of organisms dissolve in the water column before they can reach the bottom. Much of the floor of the Pacific Ocean is covered in abyssal clay.

In some areas of the abyssal substrate, potato-sized nodules of magnesium are strewn over hundreds of miles of seafloor. The mechanism that creates magnesium nodules is not completely understood, but scientists know they form as a result of a chemical reaction in the water. Some speculate that their formation is dependent on mineral-laden hot water that is spewed into the sea from deepwater hydrothermal vents.

Fig. 1.4 In a hydrothermal vent community, a black smoker (a) spews out hot water that is rich in hydrogen sulfide (b). Some of the animals that live near the vent include tube worms (c), giant clams (d), giant mussels (e), galatheid crabs (f), and (sightless) brachyuran crabs (g).

Unique Deep-Sea Environments

Although the majority of open- and deep-sea waters support few life forms, there are several unique deep-ocean marine environments that stand out as oases. These prosperous islands, many no larger than a football field, support hundreds of times as many organisms as the surrounding regions. All of these organism-rich zones share several common characteristics. Most are composed of physical structures that stand above the seafloor and therefore change the normal flow of water. Distortions in water flow can change the structure of deep-sea habitats, resulting in accumulations of sediment in some areas or upwellings of water in others. Sediment provides habitats for burrowing organisms, and upwelling increases the nutrient load in the immediate surface waters. Unique deep-sea communities form around hydrothermal vents, seamounts, and deepwater coral reefs.

In areas of the seafloor where there is geologic activity, such as volcanoes and seafloor spreading, geothermal vents may form. The first one was discovered near the Galápagos Islands in 1977, and since that time hundreds of others have been located. Along the mid-ocean ridge and in other geologically energetic regions, hot magma wells up close to the surface. Seawater that seeps through cracks in the seafloor can sink until it reaches the rocks that are located directly above the molten magma. Hydrogen sulfide and other minerals in the rocks and sediment percolate into the water as it sinks. The lava-heated rocks warm the water to 716°F (380°C), causing it to expand and spew back into the sea, forming a deep-sea vent. Although the normal boiling point of water is 212°F (100°C), water exiting these vents does not boil because it is under a tremendous amount of pressure. The boiling point of any liquid increases as pressure increases, and water pressure at these depths is extremely high.

When super-heated vent water encounters frigid oceanic water, it cools quickly. Minerals dissolved in the vent water can no longer stay in solution, and they form chimney-shaped deposits around the water outlets, as shown in the upper color insert on page C-1. The walls of the chimney grow quickly, gaining as much as 12 inches (30 cm) a day.

Eventually, the chimney becomes so tall that it falls over and then begins growing from the bottom once again. The average height of a chimney is 32.8 to 65.5 feet (10 to 20 m), although a chimney named Godzilla is 15 stories high (164 feet, or 50 m) and has an opening that is 39.4 feet (12 m) wide. Geothermal vents have very short life spans, but new ones form as older ones stop functioning. Inactive hydrothermal vents are shown in the lower color insert on page C-1.

One of the minerals in heated vent water is hydrogen sulfide, a chemical that is often associated with the rotten-egg smell of swamp mud. Hydrogen sulfide is a potent poison, as toxic to most living things as cyanide. Other minerals in the vent water include heavy metals such as iron, zinc, and copper, which can be poisonous in large doses. Despite the lethal nature of these chemicals, life flourishes around deep-sea vents. In fact, toxic hydrogen sulfide makes life around geothermal vents possible. Bacteria capable of deriving energy from hydrogen sulfide reactions support the entire geothermal vent food web.

Habitats similar to those around geothermal vents form around cold hydrocarbon seeps, places on some continental slopes where materials such as oil, methane, and hydrogen sulfide seep into the sediments. Methane gas freezes at such depths, forming deposits of methane-hydrate ice. In these ecosystems, methane, oil, and hydrogen sulfide support chemical-digesting bacteria very much like those near geothermal vents.

Another type of productive, deep-sea habitat is the seamount, an undersea volcanic mountain most often found in a geologically active region such as the edge of a tectonic plate or over a pocket of hot lava within a plate. Seamounts are similar in shape and structure to many of volcanic mountains found on the continents, with features such as rocky outcroppings, valleys, and accumulations of sediment. Many seamounts are active, lava-producing volcanoes, but others are dormant. A range of such mountains is located in the Gulf of Alaska, the largest of which is 9,900 feet (3,000 m) tall.

One of the first ones discovered was the Davidson Seamount, about 120 miles (193.1 km) southwest of Monterey, California. Formed about 12 million years ago, this now-quiet volcano is built of blocky volcanic rock with a layer of ash on the top. The waters around this highly productive structure, which is one of the largest seamounts in U.S. waters, support varied marine life, including populations of sperm whales and albatrosses.

Although coral reefs are generally associated with shallow, tropical waters, there are also coral reefs in deep, cold waters, in the Atlantic Ocean and possibly in other oceans. Unlike those that build tropical reefs, deep-sea corals require little or no light. Deep-sea coral animals and several species of sponges form dense, sediment-trapping mounds that create habitats for a variety of fish and invertebrates.

In 1998, researchers found hundreds of seabed mounds off the northwest shore of Scotland. Named the Darwin Mounds, these sandy hills support rich beds of deep-sea corals and sponges. Found at a depth of 3,280.8 feet (1,000 m) and

Kingdoms of Living Things

There are millions of different kinds of living things on Earth. To study them, scientists called taxonomists classify organisms by their characteristics. The first taxonomist was Carolus Linnaeus (1707–78), a Swedish naturalist who separated all creatures into two extremely large groups, or kingdoms: Plantae (plants) and Animalia (animals). By the middle of the 19th century, these two kingdoms had been joined by the newly designated Protista, the microscopic organisms, and Fungi. When microscopes advanced to the point that taxonomists could differentiate the characteristics of microorganisms, Protista was divided to include the kingdom Monera. By 1969, a five-kingdom classification system made up of Monera (bacteria), Protista (protozoans), Fungi, Animalia, and Plantae was established. The five-kingdom system is still in use today, although most scientists prefer to separate monerans into two groups, the kingdom Archaebacteria and the kingdom Eubacteria.

Monerans are the smallest creatures on Earth, and their cells are much simpler than the cells of other living things. Monerans that cannot make their own food are known as bacteria and include organisms such as *Escherichia coli* and *Bacillus anthracis.* Photosynthetic monerans are collectively called cyanobacteria, and include *Anabaena affinis* and *Leptolyngbya fragilis.* In the six-kingdom classification system, the most common monerans, those that live in water, soil, and on other living things, are placed in the kingdom Eubacteria. Archaebacteria are the inhabi-

spread over an area of 19.3 square miles (50 km²), the mounds are about 16.4 feet (5 m) tall and 328.1 feet (100 m) wide. Each mound is circular, with a unique, teardrop-shaped tail that extends hundreds of yards southwest of the structure. Like other deepwater structures, the mounds provide habitats for representatives from every kingdom of living things.

In 1999 scientists from the University of South Florida sighted a deepwater reef off the western coast of Florida. The reef is situated on Pulley Ridge, a submerged barrier island near Key West. It was not until 2004 that scientists were able to return to the area and confirm that the reef is alive and well. Pulley Ridge is unique for two reasons: It is the deepest reef in U.S. waters and receives just enough light to support photosynthetic organisms.

tants of extreme situations, such as hot underwater geothermal vents or extremely salty lakebeds.

Another kingdom of one-celled organisms, Protista, includes amoeba, euglena, and diatoms. Unlike monerans, protists are large, complex cells that are structurally like the cells of multicellular organisms. Members of the Protista kingdom are a diverse group varying in mobility, size, shape, and feeding strategies. A number are autotrophs, some heterotrophs, and others are mixotrophs, organisms that can make their own food and eat other organisms, depending on the conditions dictated by their environment.

The Fungi kingdom consists primarily of multicelled organisms, like molds and mildews, but there are a few one-celled members, such as the yeasts. Fungi cannot move around, and they are unable to make their own food because they do not contain chlorophyll. They are heterotrophs that feed by secreting digestive enzymes on organic material, then absorbing that material into their bodies.

The other two kingdoms, Plantae and Animalia, are also composed of multicelled organisms. Plants, including seaweeds, trees, and dandelions, do not move around but get their food by converting the Sun's energy into simple carbon compounds. Therefore, plants are autotrophs. Animals, on the other hand, cannot make their own food. These organisms are heterotrophs, and they include fish, whales, and humans, all of which must actively seek the food they eat.

Conclusion

Even though the deep sea is the Earth's largest habitat, it is largely unexplored and poorly understood. Research on marine surface waters and shallow regions has yielded knowledge about the physical and chemical conditions of the water and many of the organisms that live there. However, the difficulties of exploring the vast and remote areas make the deep ocean a frontier that still needs to be better understood.

The deep seafloor begins at the point where the continental slope plunges downward. At the base of the slope, a gentle incline called the continental rise results from the accumulation of sediment. Extending from the rise, the abyssal plain covers most of the seafloor, broken frequently with abyssal hills and occasional seamounts. The center of the ocean basin is split apart by the mid-oceanic ridge, a ring of geologically active volcanic mountains that produce new seafloor crust.

Like other parts of the ocean, the deep-sea environments are defined by factors such as salinity, temperature, density, light, pressure, currents, waves, and tides. Salinity and temperature work together to control the density of seawater. Near the poles, cold, salty surface water sinks then slides along the seafloor toward the equator. Such sinking carries oxygen to deep regions, making life possible at all depths. Sinking also sets off currents of water that result in global, thermohaline circulation. At the surface, wind generates waves and surface currents that distribute and mix the upper layers of the sea.

Most of the deep, open ocean is dark and cold. Light can only penetrate about 656.2 feet (200 m), a depth that represents only a small fraction of the total ocean water. In the upper reaches, plants and one-celled green organisms produce food. Below this photic zone, organisms must travel upward to graze or depend on food that falls down to them. Plants and animals that die sink to the seafloor, trapping vital nutrients at depths that are inaccessible to plants. Occasional upwellings of deep water bring these nutrients back to the surface and prevent their loss to the ocean ecosystem as a whole.

Several unique habitats on the deep seafloor support rich communities of living things. Geothermal vents and cold hydrocarbon sinks are places where chemicals such as hydrogen sulfide and methane reach the seawater. Specialized bacteria can convert these chemicals to energy and are able to support entire food webs. Seamounts, deepwater reefs and sand mounds also serve as hot spots for organisms such as corals, mussels, shrimp, and worms.

2

✤ Microbes and Plants
Essential Organisms in the Open Ocean

As in other ecosystems, life in the open ocean and the deep sea depends on the work of primary producers, organisms that can take advantage of an energy source and use it to make food. Most producers rely on the energy of sunlight to make food, but in many deepwater systems bacteria utilize chemicals as energy sources. In these dark realms, bacteria form the base of food chains, playing the roles that plants perform in terrestrial and shallow-water systems.

In the upper layers of the ocean where the Sun is the source of energy, primary producers are organisms that can carry out photosynthesis. Most of the photosynthetic cells in the oceanic realm live in the photic zone as members of the plankton. The term *plankton,* derived from the Greek for "wanderer" or "drifter," describes the free-floating lifestyle that characterizes these organisms. Planktonic organisms, like those in Figure 2.1, do not have anatomical features for holding onto surfaces, so they cannot attach to substrates. They also lack mechanisms for swimming, although a few types are capable of moving up and down in the water column.

The plankton community is subdivided into zooplankton, the animal-like organisms, and phytoplankton, those that contain chlorophyll. Both groups are made up of unicellular and small multicellular organisms. Phytoplankton are the most important primary producers in the marine environment as a whole. As a group, phytoplankton carry out as much photosynthesis as all of the land plants combined and are responsible for 40 percent of the photosynthesis in the sea. Composed of more than 5,000 different species, the total mass of phytoplankton exceeds that of all the marine animals combined, including fish and mammals.

Some of the dominant species of phytoplankton include tiny, green monerans, as well as green protists such as dinoflagellates, diatoms, and coccolithosphores. Most types of phytoplankton are small and transparent, qualities that make it easy for them to stay afloat but difficult for predators to see. Some avoid predators by sinking down into the aphotic zone during the day.

Zooplankton includes the larval forms of many shellfish, the eggs of both shellfish and fish, and heterotrophic bacteria and protists. Heterotrophic bacteria play roles as decomposers, nutrient recyclers, grazers, and sources of food for other organisms. Protists in the zooplankton include radiolarians, single-celled protists with shells that contain silicon, and foraminifera, single-celled organisms with carbonate shells. Many species of foraminifera also live on the deep seafloor. To survive in the upper waters, zooplankton must find food, stay afloat, and avoid larger heterotrophs.

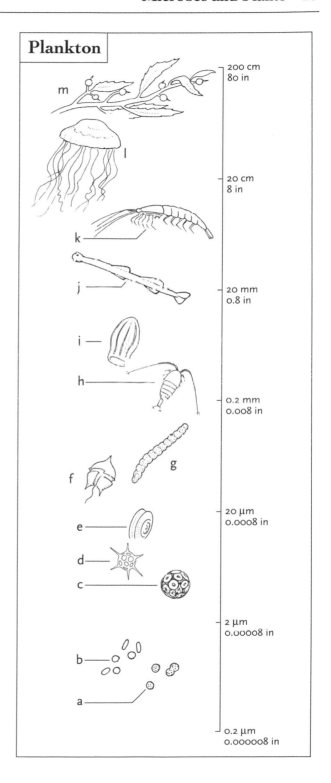

Plankton

Fig. 2.1   *Plankton includes all of the organisms that float in the surface waters. The smallest organisms are the bacteria (a) and cyanobacteria (b). Significantly larger are the one-celled coccolithophores (c), flagellates (d), diatoms (e), dinoflagellates (f), and colonial cyanobacteria (g). Copepods (h), comb jellies (i), and arrowworms (j) are some of the smallest animals that can be seen with the naked eye. Krill (k), large jellyfish (l), and floating seaweed (m) are much more obvious.*

Simple Producers

Monerans are found all over the world and as a group are the most numerous organisms on Earth. In both the water column and the sediments, populations of marine monerans are densest near the coast, dropping off as distance from the coast increases. The largest faction of photosynthesizing monerans, a group collectively known as *cyanobacteria*, contains green chlorophyll very similar to the type that is found in land plants. Each cell also holds accessory pigments, in colors of brown, gold, black, and blue-green, that enhance their ability to capture light. These pigments enable cyanobacteria to produce ample food for themselves, as well as supply food to other kinds of organisms that graze on them. Like land plants and most other green sea plants, cyanobacteria generate oxygen as a by-product of photosynthesis.

Along with cyanobacteria, a part time photosynthesizing moneran lives in the phytoplankton. Instead of depending on chlorophyll to capture the Sun's energy, these organisms contain a different kind of photosynthetic pigment called bacteriochlorophyll that can capture light waves near the infrared end of the spectrum. Unlike cyanobacteria, these monerans do not produce oxygen as a by-product of photosynthesis and are able to turn their photosynthesizing machinery on and off as needed. The ability to regulate use of bacteriochlorophyll enables these cells to use their light-capturing pigment only when food supplies are scarce in the water column. When food is plentiful, they feed like other types of heterotrophic bacteria. This dual-feeding mechanism gives bacteriochlorophyll cells a competitive edge over other types of bacteria.

A few species of open-ocean, photosynthetic cyanobacteria perform a valuable function. They capture nitrogen gas and "fix" it, making it available to other living things. Although much more abundant near shore than in deep waters, nitrogen-fixing bacteria can be found scattered throughout the oceanic realm. Because nitrogen is essential for growth and development, lack of the element often limits the number of organisms living in an environment. Nitrogen gas is abundant in both the atmosphere and in ocean water, but living things cannot use nitrogen in the gaseous form. Nitrogen-fixing bacteria

Food Chains and Photosynthesis

Living things must have energy to survive. In an ecosystem, the path that energy takes as it moves from one organism to another is called a food chain. The Sun is the major source of energy for most food chains. Organisms that can capture the Sun's energy are called producers, or autotrophs, because they are able to produce food molecules. Living things that cannot capture energy must eat food and are referred to as consumers, or heterotrophs. Heterotrophs that eat plants are herbivores, and those that eat animals are carnivores. Organisms that eat plants and animals are described as omnivores.

When living things die, another group of organisms in the food chain—the decomposers, or detritivores—uses the energy tied up in the lifeless bodies. Detritivores break down dead or decaying matter, returning the nutrients to the environment. Nutrients in ecosystems are constantly recycled through interlocking food chains called food webs. Energy, on the other hand, cannot be recycled. It is eventually lost to the system in the form of heat.

Autotrophs can capture the Sun's energy because they contain the green pigment chlorophyll. During photosynthesis, detailed in Figure 2.2, autotrophs use the Sun's energy to rearrange the carbon atoms from carbon dioxide gas to form glucose molecules. Glucose is the primary food or energy source for living things. The hydrogen and oxygen atoms needed to form glucose come from molecules of water. Producers give off the extra oxygen atoms that are generated during photosynthesis as oxygen gas.

Autotrophs usually make more glucose than they need, so they store some for later use. Heterotrophs consume this stored glucose to support their own life processes. In the long run, it is an ecosystem's productivity that determines the types and numbers of organisms that can live there.

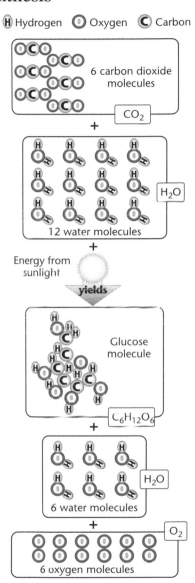

Fig. 2.2 *During photosynthesis, the energy of sunlight is used to rearrange the components of carbon dioxide and water molecules to form glucose, water, and oxygen.*

are valuable resources that convert gaseous nitrogen into a form that other living things can use. The cells that perform this task are related to species of bacteria that carry out the same job in the roots of legumes like beans. In the open ocean, species of *Synechocystis* are some of the key nitrogen fixers.

Chemoautotrophs

Although most producers are green organisms that rely on the Sun as their source of energy, a few types of monerans are classified as chemoautotrophs, organisms that can get the energy they need to make food from chemical compounds. Since these cells do not require the Sun's energy, they can operate in dark environments, like those found within sediments and at depths where sunlight cannot penetrate.

Sulfur bacteria near geothermal vents are chemoautotrophs that serve as essential parts of the deepwater food chain. These bacteria accumulate in water that slowly sinks into cracks between rocks. When the water is heated and spewed back into the ocean, the bacteria are carried along. The density of bacterial cells varies, depending on the activity of the geothermal vent. Scientists who have witnessed the formation of new vents report that the initial flurry of sulfur bacteria, and the mucus particles to which they are stuck, can create a snowlike floc thick enough to make navigation difficult.

Around geothermal vents, sulfur bacteria generate energy in a chemical reaction that converts sulfate compounds into sulfides. In many ways, this sulfur-based chemistry is similar to the chemical reaction of photosynthesis. The two primary differences are the absence of sunlight and the presence of hydrogen sulfide, H_2S. Chemoautotrophs convert hydrogen sulfide, carbon dioxide, oxygen, and water into glucose and hydrogen sulfate.

The presence of bacteria under the oceans' crust was suspected by scientists well before they were actually located. Since the discovery of deep-ocean sulfur bacteria, scientists have found other kinds of microorganisms that live on the seafloor in glasslike silica rock. Silica "glass" is a mineral formed when lava spews out of volcanic vents and cools quickly. These bacteria break down silica glass and release acid that corrodes the rock and causes pitting. To date, these microbes represent life at the lowest levels of the biosphere, the part of the Earth that supports life.

Symbiotic Monerans

Sulfur bacteria may be free-living or symbiotic. The free-living species form thick mats that coat the sides of geothermal vents. Several kinds of deep-sea animals, including crabs and fish, graze on these bacterial mats, much like terrestrial herbivores graze on grass or leaves. The mats are essential foods for many deep-sea organisms.

Symbiotic forms of sulfur bacteria establish partnerships with several kinds of animals in geothermal vent communities. *Symbiosis* refers to a relationship that forms between two different kinds of organisms. In most cases, symbiotic relationships are mutually beneficial arrangements that provide the bacterial cells with protection and housing and the host cells with food. These types of partnerships are more common in nutrient-poor waters, like those of the deep sea, than in locations where nutrients are plentiful.

Sulfur bacteria serve as symbionts within the bodies of many vent animals, including tubeworms, clams, and snails. From the safety of their positions inside the tissues of host animals, the bacteria convert hydrogen sulfide into hydrogen sulfate and use the resulting energy to make food. Even though the bacteria are making the food for their own nutrition, some of the nutrients leak out of the bacterial cells and into the tissues of the host.

Another kind of symbiotic bacteria can be found in both the open and deep oceans. Some monerans have the ability to bioluminesce, or produce light. A few of the organisms that host bioluminescent bacteria are bony fish, sharks, and protists. Unlike terrestrial environments, where bioluminescence is limited to a few species such as fireflies, many marine organisms harbor bacteria that enable them to produce their own light. Although the light of bioluminescence is soft, it is the only kind of light that most deep-sea animals ever see.

Bioluminescence

A few organisms have the ability to bioluminesce, or produce their own light. In the marine environment, light-producers include bacteria, phytoplankton, invertebrates, and fish. Bioluminescent light results from a chemical reaction that occurs within cells. A protein, luciferin, reacts with an enzyme, luciferase, in the presence of oxygen. A molecule of luciferin can only be used one time, and in most organisms new luciferin must be provided for each reaction. In some cases, luciferin and luciferase are chemically bound to one another as a large molecule called a photoprotein. Calcium and some other ions are able to trigger photoproteins to react. Most of the energy of the reaction is released as light, with very little wasted in the form of heat.

Scientists hypothesize that light-generating reactions must be important to the survival of organisms that use them because the very act of making light consumes up to 10 percent of their energy. No one knows for certain the purpose of light production, but four theories have been suggested. Light may help organisms evade their predators, attract their prey, communicate with others of their own species, or advertise. An anglerfish, which lives in deep water, where little or no light penetrates, attracts prey by dangling a glowing, lurelike appendage near its mouth. When an unsuspecting fish comes by to inspect it, the anglerfish lunges forward and engulfs it.

Flashlight fish have patches under their eyes that are filled with light-producing bacteria. The fish can control the amount of light emitted from the patches by raising or lowering lids that can cover them. These animals may use blinking signals as a form of communication, similar to the flashes produced by fireflies. A dinoflagellate, *Noctiluca,* glows when a wave or boat jostles the water, or when a fish swims nearby. The light it releases may help confuse predators swimming in its midst.

The amount of light produced by bioluminescence is significant. Even though the glow from a single dinoflagellate lasts only 0.1 seconds, it is visible to the human eye. Larger organisms, like jellyfish, emit greater quantities of light. Jellyfish and other large organisms may glow for tens of seconds.

Most of the light produced by living things is blue. Underwater blue light can travel farther than any other color, so light produced in shades of blue is carried the greatest possible distance. In addition, most marine organisms are adapted to see shades of blue but are blind to other colors. An exception to this rule is a fish known as loosejaw that gives off, and is capable of seeing, red light. Humans cannot see the glow of loosejaws because the shade of red it emits is close to the infrared portion of the electromagnetic spectrum. This fish may be better camouflaged than any other bioluminescent organism since it produces a light that helps it see its own species and possibly its prey, while it cannot be seen by other organisms.

Heterotrophic Bacteria and Fungi

Not all kinds of the bacteria are producers. Species that cannot make their own food must ingest their nutrition. Heterotrophic bacteria feed on a variety of materials, including dead or decaying plants and animals, cyanobacteria, other heterotrophic bacteria, and dissolved nutrients. As a group, heterotrophic bacteria are vitally important to the process of decomposition. By breaking down complex compounds to secure their own nutrients, they release valuable inorganic materials such as phosphorous and nitrogen to the environment. In addition, heterotrophic bacteria serve as a source of food for organisms like protozoans and small shellfish.

Heterotrophic bacteria are vital components of microscopic food webs known as microbial loops. When surface-dwelling organisms die, some of the organic material in their bodies begins to sink to the seafloor. Much of that organic material dissolves in the seawater and becomes part of the dissolved organic matter (DOM). In addition, one-celled autotrophs secrete energy-rich compounds called mucopolysaccharides, which serve as another important source of DOM. Heterotrophic bacteria can absorb DOM and use it as efficiently as any other source of food. These bacteria are then fed on by heterotrophic protists, which in turn serve as food for tiny invertebrates. In this way heterotrophic bacteria act as a bridge between larger organisms in the food chain and valuable dissolved nutrients in the water. Without heterotrophic bacteria, most of the nutrients in DOM would be lost to the upper-water food webs.

In open-ocean conditions, some of the decomposition of *detritus* is done by fungi. There are about 500 species of fungi in the marine environment. Like bacteria, fungi break down organic matter and change it into simpler materials for their own use, releasing some nutrients and minerals into the environment. Marine fungi grow across dead and decaying plant and animal matter by extending thin filaments called *hyphae*. Each fungal filament releases enzymes that dissolve the tissues of the wood, converting them to a liquid form for easy absorption.

Fungi can reproduce sexually or asexually. Sexually, cells of two different mating types form a mating bridge between them. The nucleus of one cell crosses the bridge to fuse with the nucleus of the other cell, combining the *DNA* of the two.

The structure that grows from this cell can develop into a fruiting body. Asexual spores produced by the fruiting bodies generate new fungi. In some cases, spores are also produced by structures that arise from asexual cells of fungi. In marine fungi, spores show special adaptations, such as appendages, that either help them float or enable them to cling to substrates.

Protists

Hundreds of species of protists live among the bacteria in the plankton. Many, such as diatoms, dinoflagellates, and coccolithophores, are producers, responsible for much of the open-sea photosynthesis. Others, including foraminiferans and radiolarians, are consumers.

Diatoms are protists that are most commonly found in cool marine waters. The distinctive gold-brown color of diatoms is due to a combination of chlorophyll and a golden brown pigment. There are many species of diatoms, but all share some common traits. Diatoms are unicellular organisms that build silica shells called frustules around themselves. Some are round, and their two-part frustules look like the lids and bases of microscopic pillboxes. Others are long and narrow, a shape that is described as pinnate.

Like many protists, diatoms can reproduce *asexually* by *binary fission*. In this process, a parent cell divides into two identical daughter cells. In diatoms, one daughter cell receives the top, and larger, portion of the parent frustule and the other receives the smaller bottom piece. Once division is complete, both daughters treat the portion they inherited as their own top and grow new lower pieces. As a result, one of the daughter cells is smaller than the other. Cells either undergo a period of growth to regain their normal size and produce new frustules, or they go through *sexual reproduction*.

Sexual reproduction can be accomplished by more than one method. A small diatom cell may break into pieces, each of which swims around until it locates and fuses with another diatom cell. The product of their fusion builds the new frustule. Or, two adult diatom cells can line up side by side. After each cell undergoes binary fission, the two exchange one daughter

Advantages of Sexual Reproduction

Even though asexual reproduction seems like a simple solution to continuing a species, many monerans and protists also undergo sexual reproduction. While asexual reproduction expands a population, it does not make it possible for the population to change in any way. All of the organisms created in asexual reproduction are clones, so they have the same genetic information and the same characteristics as the parent organism. As long as environmental conditions remain steady, asexual reproduction maintains a healthy population; however, if anything in the environment changes, the population may suddenly be at risk. Because all the individuals are alike, any problem that may befall one cell will probably visit them all, possibly resulting in the loss of the entire population.

In organisms that reproduce sexually, all of the offspring are different. Each one contains a unique set of genetic information, half of it inherited from one parent and half from the other. Since individuals in the population vary, it is unlikely that a change in the environment would create problems for everyone. In fact, a change that reduces the survival rate of some might improve the survival rate of others.

cell. The new pairs of daughter cells fuse, resulting in two new cells, each possessing genetic material from two parents.

Diatoms serve as food for a large number of organisms, including members of the zooplankton. Each diatom cell is held up in the water column by a drop of oil for *buoyancy* and structures like extensions and whorls that help prevent the cells from sinking. Diatoms that are not consumed by predators eventually die and their shells fall to the seafloor. Centuries of accumulated mud and sediment that contain these diatom shells, known as diatomaceous earth, is mined for use as a filter or abrasive.

Dinoflagellates are more common in warm, tropical waters than diatoms. Possessing pigments that give them colors varying from red to green, dinoflagellates blur the distinction between producer and consumer. If food supplies in the water are ample, the protists either absorb organic matter or capture bacteria. However, when resources are low, the organisms make their own food.

A free-living dinoflagellate is protected by its smooth, flexible armor made of cellulose. Two *flagella* help propel the protist through the water. Many species also have bristlelike extensions that protrude from their armor and serve two purposes: to prevent the cells from sinking and to discourage predators.

When environmental conditions are just right, dinoflagellates and several other kinds of algae and protists reproduce rapidly, yielding dense populations of organisms that are collectively known as an *algal bloom*. As populations of microbes increase, the water changes color, the exact shade of which depends on the species of organisms present. Red is a common color for blooms that contain large numbers of dinoflagellates and has led to the general designation of "red tide" for any algal bloom. Scientists prefer to call such events harmful algal blooms (HABs), since tides are not involved in the phenomena and colors can vary from green to brown.

Algal blooms pose two threats to aquatic life: They can use up all of the oxygen in the water and some manufacture toxins. Autotrophs like dinoflagellates generate oxygen during the day as a by-product of photosynthesis, but at night oxygen production stops. In the process of respiration, a day and night activity, algal cells consume oxygen. When populations of cells are extremely large, oxygen supplies in the water can be depleted at night, causing the death of the algae as well as other oxygen-dependent organisms like fish and shellfish. Only a few of the more than 1,000 species of dinoflagellates are capable of producing toxins. Although the toxins do not harm shellfish that feed on the dinoflagellates, they can be fatal to fish, birds, marine mammals, and humans that consume the shellfish or fish.

Like most species of protists, dinoflagellates usually reproduce asexually by binary fission. In the armored species, each daughter cell gets half of the armor, then each makes the other half of its shell. Sexual reproduction occurs when two cells fuse to form a single, large cell that contains the DNA of both parental cells. The large cell splits into two daughter cells, each with new combinations of DNA.

Another group of photosynthetic protists, the coccolithophores, are organisms covered with microscopic calcium carbonate plates. Like many other types of phytoplankton, dense populations of coccolithophores live at the surface of the water. One species, *Emiliania huxleyi,* or Ehux, is found worldwide except for polar climates. During blooms, billions of white Ehux cells can give thousands of square miles of ocean surface water a milky turquoise appearance. When the organisms die, their coccoliths accumulate in thick layers on the seafloor.

Other kinds of protists that live in oceanic waters include amoebalike organisms such as foraminiferans and radiolarians. Unlike diatoms, dinoflagellates, and coccolithophores, "forams" and radiolarians do not contain chlorophyll. For this reason, they are consumers and members of the zooplankton. Both types of cells feed by absorbing nutrients from the water and by engulfing tiny bits of food.

Depending on the species, foraminiferans float in the water or live in the sediment. They move by sending out extensions of their cytoplasm ("false feet," or pseudopods) through tiny holes in their shells. Pseudopods enable them to inch their way along substrates. Radiolarians are also amoeboid protists, but their tests, or shells, are made of silica. The tests of radiolarians are studded with tiny spines and other projections to deter predators. Holes in the tests enable the organisms to extend pseudopods to capture food.

One group of protists, the ciliates, is made up of cells that are covered in short, hairlike structures called *cilia.* The beating motion of cilia provides these cells with weak locomotion but also sweeps food particles toward their mouth-like oral grooves. Ciliates can be found in many different parts of the environment, including the water column, the substrate, and attached to the gills of several kinds of animals. As predators, they usually feed on monerans. By doing so, ciliates make the nutrition contained in the extremely small moneran cells available to members of the food chain that cannot feed directly on such tiny prey.

Protists and bacteria that live on the water's surface contribute to an important deep-sea marine phenomenon known as marine snow. In the food-manufacturing process, green cells "leak" compounds called mucopolysaccharides. These are often produced as sticky strings, very much like spider webs, that cling to anything they touch. As they float in the upper waters, the strings adhere to other matter, such as fecal pellets and bits of dead and decaying plant and animal material. Eventually, the growing mass becomes heavy enough to sink and begins a slow downward drift to the seafloor far below, very much like a fat snowflake drifts to the ground. When surface productivity is high, particles of marine snow can resemble a blizzard. On the seafloor, these clumps of organic matter provide food for a variety of organisms, including many bottom-dwelling bacteria.

Giant Protists

Most protists are tiny organisms, invisible to the naked eye. However, the xenophyophores are a group of giant protists that measure up to 9.8 inches (25 cm) in diameter. One species, *Syringammina fragilissima,* can be found in all oceans, but is most common in benthic deep-sea habitats. Xenophyophores have tests that they construct by gluing sediment grains together. Inside each test is the organism, a multinucleate mass of protoplasm that is surrounded by a system of stiff tubes.

Syringammina fragilissima feeds by extending its pseudopods through the test to collect particles of organic matter suspended in the water. The organism also takes advantage of bacteria that grow within its tests. Outside the protist's protoplasm, but inside its test, pellets of feces accumulate in sticky masses. Bacteria attach to these masses of feces and feed on them, quickly coating their surfaces. When the bacterial populations on these masses become dense, *Syringammina fragilissima* ingests them, fecal pellets and all. In such a harsh environment where food is scarce, organisms cannot afford to ignore any source.

The color and shape of tests belonging to *Syringammina fragilissima* vary, depending on the type of soil in the sediment, geographic location, and the presence or absence of deep-sea water currents. Some cells produce rounded tests that resemble bath sponges, while others form flattened disks or branched tubes. Because the tests are porous, perforated with large holes, the organisms inside use them to trap food particles.

Differences in Terrestrial and Aquatic Plants

Even though plants that live in water look dramatically different from terrestrial plants, the two groups have a lot in common. Both types of plants capture the Sun's energy and use it to make food from raw materials. In each case, the raw materials required include carbon dioxide, water, and minerals. The differences in these two types of plants are adaptations to their specific environments.

Land plants are highly specialized for their lifestyles. They get their nutrients from two sources: soil and air. It is the job of roots to absorb water and minerals from the soil, as well as hold the plant in place. Essential materials are transported to cells in leaves by a system of tubes called vascular tissue. Leaves are in charge of taking in carbon dioxide gas from the atmosphere for photosynthesis. Once photosynthesis is complete, a second set of vascular tissue carries the food made by the leaves to the rest of the plant. Land plants are also equipped with woody stems and branches that hold them upright so that they can receive plenty of light.

Marine plants, called macroalgae or seaweeds, get their nutrients, water, and dissolved gases from seawater. Since water surrounds the entire marine plant, these dissolved nutrients simply diffuse into each cell. For this reason, marine plants do not have vascular tissue to accommodate photosynthesis or to carry its products to each cell. In addition, marine plants do not need support structures because they are held up by the buoyant force of the water. Since water in the ocean is always moving, the bodies of marine plants are flexible, permitting them to go with that movement. Some marine plants secrete mucus to make their surfaces slick, further reducing their drag or resistance to water movement. Mucus also helps keep animals from eating them.

A plant that grows on land is described with terms such as *leaf, stem,* and *root.* Seaweeds are made up of different components. The parts of seaweed that look like leaves are termed *blades,* or fronds. Some are equipped with small, gas-filled sacs, or *bladders,* that help keep them afloat and close to the sunlight. The gases in these bladders are usually nitrogen, argon, and oxygen. The stemlike structures of macroalgae are referred to as *stipes.* A root-shaped mass, the *holdfast,* anchors seaweeds but does not absorb nutrients like true roots do. Together, the blades, stipes, and holdfast make up the body, or *thallus,* of the macroalgae. Thalli take on many different forms, including tall and branched or thin and flat.

Underneath nutrient-rich surface waters, populations of *Syringammina fragilissima* can be dense, reaching 2,000 organisms in an area of 120 square yards (100 m²). In these cases, the protists are the dominant organisms in the local habitats. As a group, they enrich the waters above the seafloor by stirring up benthic particles, re-suspending organic matter that has settled. The tests of *Syringammina fragilissima* provide homes for small worms as well as filter-feeding and deposit-feeding shellfish.

Brown Algae

Very few algae make their homes in the deep, open sea. Most algae need a point of attachment and prefer shallow waters that provide them with hard substrates and plenty of sunlight. One brown alga, sargassum weed, is an exception, and can be found covering much of the surface of the Atlantic Ocean.

Sargassum and sargassum weed are common names for macroalgae in the genus *Sargassum,* which contains more than 500 species worldwide. Individual plants have yellow-brown leaves attached to dark brown stipes and may develop to be 19.6 feet (6 m) long. Early in life, the plants grow from holdfasts that secure them to the bottom, but many break loose and float freely to the deep sea. Large clumps of sargassum, called rafts or "weed bands," accumulate where currents come together.

Several adaptations of sargassum weed enable this plant to flourish on the high seas. The plants are flexible and able to move with the flow of water because stipes and fronds synthesize a gel-like coating called alginate. To maintain their positions at the surface of the water, fronds are equipped with gas-filled air bladders that act like floats.

Sargassum mats provide habitats for unique communities of organisms in the surface waters of the deep ocean. A meadow of sargassum offers protection from predators and cover from the elements. Microbes that accumulate on the plants serve as food for small organisms.

Sargasso Sea

The 2,000,000 square mile (5,179,976.22 km^2) Sargasso Sea is the only sea in the world that has no coastlines. Located in the northwest Atlantic Ocean between the West Indies and the Azores, the Sargasso Sea is wedged between the Gulf Stream on the western side and the North Equatorial Current on the eastern side. These streams of moving water gently rotate the sea in a clockwise direction.

Early Portuguese sailors gave the sea its name because the air bladders on the sargassum weeds reminded them of *sargaco,* the Portuguese word for grapes. The sea gained an unfortunate reputation among sailors because it is located in a very calm area that often experiences little or no wind. Early sailors mistakenly believed that their slow progress through the area was caused by sargassum weed clinging to their ships. A group of

Spanish sailors nicknamed the sea the "Horse Latitudes," because they found themselves stranded there in calm, windless weather and had to throw their horses overboard to conserve water.

The Sargasso Sea is a nutrient-poor body of water that has been compared to a desert ecosystem. Like a desert, this sea supports its own, unique communities of organisms. Living in and among the sargassum weed are countless small animals including fish, shellfish, and octopuses. Some are highly specialized to blend in with the weeds. Many others, especially the poor swimmers, are dependent on the seaweed to stay afloat. Most of the animals that live there do not graze on the sargassum weed, which has a tough, rubbery texture. Instead, animals of the Sargasso Sea are omnivores that prey on smaller animals or eat dead and decaying matter.

Conclusion

Unlike most ecosystems on Earth, the food webs of deep- and open-sea environments involve very few plants. Within the photic zone, green one-celled monerans and protists are the key primary producers. Plants are virtually absent, with only one species, *Sargassum,* playing any role. Phytoplankton, including cyanobacteria, protists, diatoms, and coccolithophores, are responsible for producing the food that supports the majority of oceanic food chains. In recent years scientists have added a new primary producer, a bacterium equipped with bacteriochlorophyll, to the short list of energy makers.

Zooplankton living among the phytoplankton are the second link in the open-ocean food chain. Heterotrophic bacteria and protists live among other floating consumers such as shellfish larvae and not fully developed fish. By feeding on primary producers, zooplankton make the energy they capture available to other organisms.

In the dark waters of the hydrothermal vent communities, sunlight is lacking and all primary production is carried out by sulfur bacteria, a type of chemoautotroph. Sulfur bacteria extract energy from a chemical reaction in which sulphides are converted into sulphates; the energy gained in this process is used to make simple sugars such as *glucose*. These bacteria originate from under the seafloor's crust and represent some of the newest monerans studied by scientists.

Sulfur bacteria may be free-living or symbiotic. The free-living species form mats on the substrates around the thermal vents. Symbiotic forms live inside the tissues of animals, including clams and worms.

Many open-ocean and deep-sea animals also establish symbiotic relationships with bioluminescent bacteria. Bioluminescence is a chemical reaction that produces light. Organisms such as dinoflagellates and fish support light-emitting bacteria.

3

Sponges, Cnidarians, and Worms
Animals of the Ocean Surface and Seafloor

The largest portion of the ocean is the open, deepwater area beyond the edges of the continental shelf. More than 88 percent of the ocean is deeper than one mile (1.6 km). The open sea and the deep seafloor are *difficult* environments that pose unique problems to living things. At the surface of the open ocean, marine animals have no place to hide from predators or seek protection from the Sun. In addition, nutrients in the upper levels of water are patchy, with only a small percentage of ocean area capable of supporting colonies of phytoplankton. Consequently, there are not many places where large numbers of animals can be found. In those rare zones where they do exist, populations of a few species flourish, but the species diversity is relatively low.

Deepwater animals face an entirely different set of conditions than those in the upper layers. Light is absent, temperatures are frigid, and the water pressure is extremely high. Populations of deep-sea organisms are sparse, except in a few patchy areas that are referred to as "hot spots." In these regions, the diversity of organisms is very high, but the numbers of individuals in each population are low.

In deep water one of the most difficult challenges is the extremely high pressure. At sea level, air pressure is about one atmosphere, or 14.7 pounds per square inch. This means that when a person is standing at the beach, a column of air weighing 14.7 pounds presses down on each square inch of their body. The pressure of water is much greater than the pressure of air, because water is heavier. With every 33-foot (10 m) descent in the water, hydrostatic pressure increases by one atmosphere. At 3,300 feet (1,000 m), the hydrostatic pressure on an organism is 1,500 pounds per square inch (510 kg/cm²), or about 100 times more pressure than at the

Biodiversity

Biodiversity, or biological diversity, refers to the variety of living things in an area. Diversity is higher in complex environments than in simple ones. Complex physical environments have a lot to offer organisms in the way of food and housing. Estuaries, shorelines, and coral reefs are extremely complex marine environments, and each of them provides a wide assortment of nutritional resources for living things.

There are thousands of habitats in estuaries, coastal systems where fresh and salt water meet and mix. The bottom of the estuary provides homes for different kinds of organisms. Some spend their entire lives on the surface of the sediment, many burrow just under the surface, and others dig deep into the sediment. Organisms also select locations that accommodate their abilities to tolerate salt, so those that are adapted to high salinity are on the seaward side while the freshwater-dependent ones are on the river side. In between the two extremes, organisms live in zones that meet the salinity requirements for their bodies.

Diversity is an important aspect of a healthy ecosystem. In an ecosystem where all living things are exactly the same, one big change in the environment could cause widespread destruction. This might be best understood in a familiar ecosystem, like a forest. If only one kind of tree is growing in the forest, a virus that damages that type of plant could wipe out the entire forest. If the forest contains 20 different kinds of trees, it is unlikely that one disease agent could destroy the entire plant community. A high degree of biodiversity gives an ecosystem an edge, ensuring that it can continue to exist and function regardless of changes around it.

surface. At depths of 35,000 feet (10,600 m), pressure increases to 7.5 tons per square inch (5,100 kg/cm^2). Even though a human diver would be crushed to death at such pressures, deep-sea animals thrive. Their bodies are physically adapted for life at the bottom of the sea.

Invertebrates, animals that do not have backbones, are the most numerous organisms in the open and deep ocean. Scientists estimate that the number of invertebrate marine species runs into the millions and that many invertebrates have not even been discovered yet. Some marine invertebrates are *sessile* organisms, nonmotile creatures that spend most of their lives in one place. Nutritionally, most of these are classified as either filter or suspension feed-ers. Filter feeders strain bits of organic matter from the seawater, while sus-pension feeders scoop up sediment and extract organic material from it. Other invertebrates are motile preda-tors that capture small animals either by pursuing or by ambushing them.

Some of the simplest invertebrates are sponges, cnidarians, and worms. The majority of them are bottom-dwellers, although jellyfish and some types of worms live in the water col-umn. As a group, simple invertebrates are highly successful organisms that have been on Earth much longer than the more advanced animals.

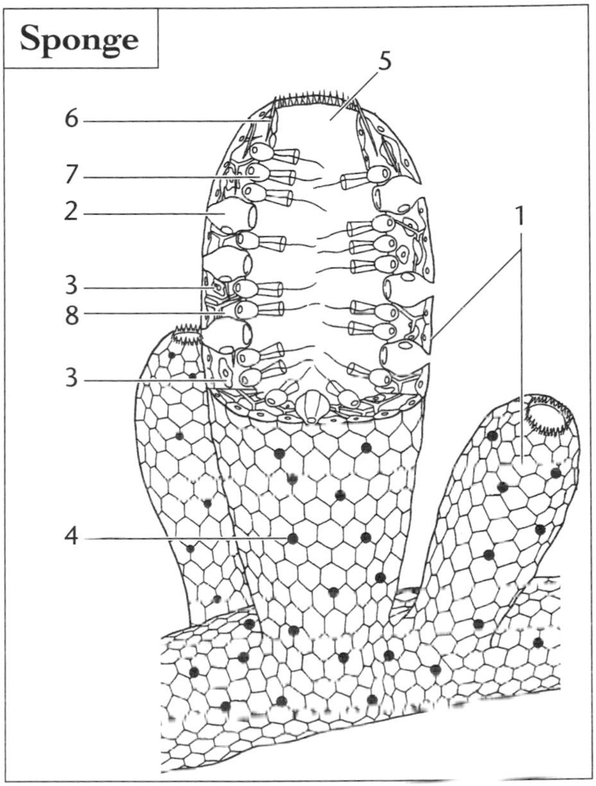

Sponges

Sponges are the oldest and most prim-itive group of animals. Traces of sponges have been found in fossil rocks that date back 600 million years. During their long existence on Earth, sponges have survived many global extinctions, events that completely eliminated other types of animals.

The sponges found in today's oceans are very similar to their ancestors. Barely more than colonies of cells, these animals lack organized tissues and organ systems. A sponge's body, shown in Figure 3.1, is designed very much like a two-layered sack. The

Fig. 3.1   *The epidermis (1) of a sponge is filled with tiny pores called porocytes (2). Amoebocytes (3) move around the sponge carrying food to cells. Water enters the sponge through an incurrent pore (4), flows into the central cavity, and exits through the osculum (5). Spicules (6) lend support to the sponge's body wall. Choanocytes (7) lash their flagella in the central cavity to keep water moving through the sponge and to gather bits of food that are suspended in the water. The mesoglea (8) is a jellylike matrix located between the epidermis and the cells that line the central cavity.*

outer layer of the sack, or *epidermis*, is in contact with the environment, and the inner layer, the *gastrodermis*, lines the stomach cavity. Between these two layers is a jellylike matrix called the *mesoglea*.

Although sponges do not have skeletons, their bodies are supported by hard needlelike structures called *spicules* that are scattered throughout the mesoglea. Depending on the type of sponge, spicules can be made of either calcium carbonate or silica. Some species possess fibers made of a tough rubbery protein called spongin instead of hard spicules.

Scientists divide sponges into four large classes based on the composition of their spicules: Calcarea, Hexactinellida, Demospongia, and Sclerospongia. Calcarea, named for their hard, calcium carbonate spicules, are usually small. Hexactinellida, also small sponges, have silica spicules resembling threads of glass, giving the group the common name of glass sponges. The body of a glass sponge is unique because it is made up of one big cell instead of millions of small cells, as in other animals. Nuclei are spread throughout the cellular mass, but no cell membranes separate them. The familiar bath sponges, class Demospongia, are larger than most other types of sponges, and their exoskeletons are not as hard because their spicules are made of spongin. Sclerospongia sponges produce heavy calcium carbonate skeletons and play an important role in the formation of reefs.

A sponge draws water into its body through tiny pores in the body wall. *Chaonocytes,* flagellated cells lining the gastrodermis, pull water through the pores, into the central cavity, and out one or more openings called oscula. Flagella also collect food particles that are suspended in the water. Food is broken down into nutrients within cells of the gastrodermis. Nutrients are picked up by mobile amoeboid cells that carry them to all parts of the sponge.

A sponge lacks specialized structures for extracting oxygen from the water. Because all of its cells are in contact with seawater, oxygen simply diffuses into each one. Carbon dioxide, a waste product of cellular activity, diffuses out of the cells and into the water.

Reproduction can occur sexually or asexually in sponges. Sexually, all sponges are *hermaphrodites,* producing both male and female sex cells. Depending on the species, either sperm or both sperm and eggs are released into the water. In either case, the gametes find one another, fuse, and form zygotes. Zygotes develop into *larvae* that swim in the water column for a short time before settling to the bottom to begin their sessile mature lives. Once attached to a substrate, sponges remain there for the rest of their lives.

A sponge can also reproduce asexually by forming buds, small organisms that grow at the base of the parent sponge. When buds are mature, they separate from the parent and live independently. In addition, sponges have tremendous powers of regeneration, enabling each piece of a sponge that is torn apart by waves to develop into a new organism.

Since sponges are stationary, they may seem like easy targets for hungry predators. In reality, sponges are not defenseless. Many animals that attempt to dine on sponges are repelled by painful pricks from needlelike spicules. In other cases, predators are repelled by chemicals that either taste foul or contain toxins.

Because adult sponges must attach to firm substrates, they compete with anemones and corals for space. In deep water, where sponges are not constantly bombarded by the high energy of waves, they grow large and take on the shapes of barrels, vases, shelves, flowers, or branching plants. Since they are animals and as such do not require light to grow, sponges can be found at all depths of the seafloor.

Glass sponges, normally found in waters along the continental slopes to depths of 23,000 feet (7,000 m), have been the objects of much research. Sally Leys and George O. Mackie of the University of Alberta have found that one species of these one-celled sponges (*Rhabdocalyptus dawsoni*) can respond to danger by generating electrical signals. In laboratory experiments, glass sponges stopped moving their flagella when they were touched. The signal to stop flagella is transmitted throughout the sponge along a network of fine filaments, and it may function to protect the sponge from pulling sandy water into its pores, clogging them.

There are two types of glass sponges: the soft, non-reef-forming species and the hard, reef-forming types. By attaching to the substrate and to one another, reef-forming glass sponges create strong, deep-sea structures that resemble glass

Body Symmetry

An important characteristic of the body plan of an animal is its symmetry. Symmetry refers to the equivalence in size and shape of sections of an animal's body. Most animals exhibit body symmetry, but a few species of sponges are asymmetrical. If a plane were passed through the body of an asymmetrical sponge, slicing it in two, the parts would not be the same.

Some animals are radially symmetrical. Shaped like either short or long cylinders, these stationary or slow-moving organisms have distinct top and bottom surfaces but lack fronts and backs, heads or tails. A plane could pass through a radially symmetrical animal in several places to create two identical halves. Starfish, jellyfish, sea cucumbers, sea lilies, and sand dollars are a few examples of radially symmetrical animals.

The bodies of most animals are bilaterally symmetrical, a form in which a plane could pass through the animal only in one place to divide it into two equal parts. The two halves of a bilaterally symmetrical animal are mirror images of each other. Bilateral symmetry is associated with animals that move around. The leading part of a bilaterally symmetrical animal's body contains sense organs such as eyes and nose. Fish, whales, birds, snakes, and humans are all bilaterally symmetrical.

Scientists have special terms to describe the body of a bilaterally symmetrical animal. The head or front region is called the anterior portion and the opposite end, the hind region, is the posterior. The stomach or underside is the ventral side, and opposite that is the back, or dorsal, side. Structures located on the side of an animal are described as lateral.

walls. Glass sponge reefs are similar in structure to those built by corals. As each generation of sponges dies, a new generation builds on top of the skeletons. Glass-sponge reefs favor fast-moving, deep, cold water that carries a high concentration of silica. The rushing water delivers oxygen and food to the stationary sponges. Glass sponges also prefer locations where sediment falls out of water very slowly. Although some sediment around glass sponges helps to strengthen their reef structures, too much can bury the entire reef.

In the relatively barren deep ocean, glass-sponge reefs play an important role as habitats, places for animals to eat and live. The reefs provide substrates to which other kinds of animals can attach, as well as hiding and nesting sites. During one research dive, scientists counted 17,000 organisms, including crabs, shrimp, and fish, living inside of one glass sponge.

The Venus flower basket (*Euplectella*) is a glass sponge that can be found in deep Pacific waters, most often sharing a symbiotic relationship with shrimp. When they are tiny and immature, shrimp swim through the network of silica spicules to enter a Venus flower basket. Inside, they feed on the plankton in water that the sponge constantly draws through its body. Because the sponge offers protection from predators, the shrimp are safer inside of it than in the open water. As the shrimp grow, they eventually become too large to swim out of the sponge and are permanently trapped there.

Cnidarians

Jellyfish, corals, anemones, and sea fans share similar physical and chemical characteristics and are classified as cnidarians. The sack like bodies of cnidarians are fringed with tentacles that are armed with stinging cells. As shown in Figure 3.2,

Fig. 3.2 Cnidarians have two body plans, a vase-shaped polyp (a) and a bell-shaped medusa (b). Each body plan is equipped with tentacles (1), a gastrovascular cavity (2), and a single body opening, the mouth (3).

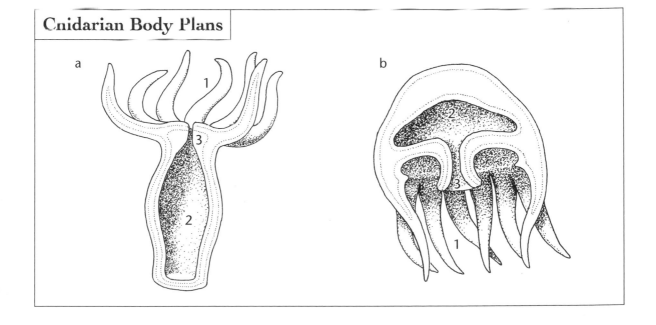

Cnidarian Body Plans

a

b

cnidarians exhibit two body forms, medusa, or polyp. Medusas are bell-shaped, like the bodies of jellyfish. Polyps are vase-shaped animals that attach to submerged surfaces. In general, polyps are part of the benthos, whereas medusas float or swim in the water column. In many species, cnidarians go through both the polyp and medusa stages in their life cycles.

Cnidarians are slightly more complex than sponges. Like a sponge, the body walls of cnidarians are made of outer and inner layers, with a mesoglea between them. Unlike a sponge, a cnidarian has a mouth ringed with tentacles, which are responsible for taking in food and expelling wastes. A simple network of nerves runs through the body, extending down through the tentacles to specialized cells called *cnidocytes*. Used in defense and in capturing food, each cnidocyte is armed with a *nematocyst,* a hooked structure attached to a long filament. When triggered, the nematocyst uncoils and shoots out its barbed tip. In some species, the tips contain poisons that can paralyze or kill prey, and in others they are covered with sticky mucus. Once an item is snared, tentacles move it through the cnidarian's mouth and into the gastrovascular cavity.

Scientists separate cnidarians into three classes: Anthozoa, Hydrozoa, and Scyphozoa. Class Anthozoa contains corals, sea fans, anemones, sea pens, and gorgonians. The class Hydrozoa includes a group of colonial animals known as hydroids. Scyphozoan, the only true jellyfish of the three, may be the most familiar class.

The anthozoans spend their lives as sessile polyps that range in size from a fraction of an inch to more than three feet (1 m) in diameter, depending on the species. Corals, typical anthozoans, are capable of both sexual and asexual reproduction. In sexual reproduction, male and female reproductive tissues release eggs and sperm into the water. Fertilized eggs develop into swimming larvae, each about the size of the head of a pin. Larvae swim some distance before settling to the bottom and permanently attaching to the substrate. A young coral may reproduce asexually by forming buds, tiny clones that grow from its base. In this way, the original polyp can form a colony of polyps.

For protection, some species of coral secrete cup-shaped skeletons of calcium carbonate, or limestone. As each polyp grows, it continuously adds to its skeleton. Young polyps frequently attach to the skeletons of dead polyps, building on the structures created by their ancestors. In this way, they form extensive reefs of calcium carbonate.

A deep-sea coral can feed in several ways. When small fish and other prey are available, the coral subdues them with stings from nematocysts, then moves the food into its mouth. The tentacles are capable of picking up small bits of detritus in the water and using them for food. Corals can also absorb dissolved organic matter (DOM) directly from the water.

Fig. 3.3 Oculina varicosa *can be found in deep water off the coast of Florida.* (Courtesy of The Coral Kingdom Collection, NOAA)

Although most deep-sea corals are solitary, a few species of hard corals form reefs. One of the most abundant reef-forming corals in deep water is *Oculina varicosa*, a branching, ivory-colored species seen in Figure 3.3. This slow-growing cnidarian can produce limestone structures as tall as 98.4 feet (30 m). *Oculina varicosa* are the primary corals in a reef off the eastern coast of Florida called the Oculina Banks.

Lophelia is another cold-water coral that forms reefs. Although usually found between 657 and 3,300 feet (200 and 1,000 m), this coral can be found as deep as 9,843 feet (3,000 m). *Lophelia* is a suspension feeder that catches detritus and plankton in the water. In the deep ocean, *Lophelia* reefs are thousands of years old, and some have grown to heights of 600 feet (183 m).

Spawning and Brooding

For sexual reproduction to take place, male and female cells must come together. Many marine species spawn, or discharge one or both of their sex cells into the water. For this strategy to be successful, eggs and sperm must be released at the same time, which is why spawning usually occurs once a year at a specific time. Animals are cued to release gametes by specific environmental factors, such as the Moon's phase, length of daylight, or temperature.

The alternative strategy to spawning is brooding. Animals that brood release sperm into the water, while eggs remain within the mother. Sperm swim around until they find a female, enter her body, and fertilize the eggs. Eggs are brooded within the mother's body until time for them to hatch.

Fertilized eggs that are brooded have the advantage of protection from predators during development. In comparison, eggs fertilized in the water column or on the seafloor are at high risk from predators. For this reason, animals that brood their developing eggs only produce small numbers of gametes, while those that spawn discharge hundreds of thousands of gametes, a strategy that ensures that a few of the resulting offspring will survive until adulthood.

The reefs formed by hard, deepwater corals like *Oculina* and *Lophelia* are referred to by a variety of names, including mounds, banks, groves, and thickets. Some of these cold-water structures are the largest reefs in the world, exceeding the size of lush, tropical coral reefs. In the deep oceans, reefs provide structures that support other anthozoans like black corals, gorgonians, sea fans, and sea pens. Reefs also provide habitats for other kinds of animals. The kinds of corals that form the Darwin Mounds in the Atlantic Ocean include *Lophelia pertusa* as well as other cold-water corals such as *Madrepora aculata* and *Solenosmilia variabilis.*

Anemones are cnidarians that exist in the polyp form, like hard corals, but they lack skeletal structures. The body of an anemone has two distinct ends. The upper end of the polyp is the oral disk, a mouth surrounded by tentacles, and the other end is a suction-cup-like disk that holds the animal to the substrate. Anemones are usually stationary, but some move by sliding on the substrate on their basal disk, somersaulting on their tentacles or floating to a new location.

Reproduction in anemones occurs sexually and asexually. In the sexual phase, both eggs and sperm are released into the water. The sperm of one animal swim into the gastric cavity of another and fertilize its eggs, which develop into larvae that swim out of the parent's mouth. After a short time in the plankton, larvae settle to the bottom to grow into adult anemones. Asexual reproduction occurs by longitudinal fission, a process in which the organism splits down the middle to form two separate individuals.

The burrowing anemone, *Cerianthus borealis*, resembles a short palm tree. Living in the sediments of deep water, the elongated body of *Cerianthus borealis* digs its column into the mud and then builds a mucus and mud tube around itself. Another tube-dwelling species, *Pachycerianthus fimbriatus*, quickly retreats into its hard tube when threatened.

One group of corals is commonly known as the "black" or "horny" corals because their dense, black skeletons are made of material similar to horn. In reef-forming corals, the living tissue is protected inside the skeleton, but in black corals the tissue is located on the outside. Most black corals live in deep, tropical waters where they grow upright, looking very much like small, gnarled trees.

The octocorals or gorgonians are colonies of soft coral polyps, each with eight tentacles, as shown in the photo. A colony of octocorals is housed inside a protective matrix that gives it a plant like appearance. In many species, the protective covering is flexible and fleshy, with hornlike, or crystalline, support structures spread throughout. This group

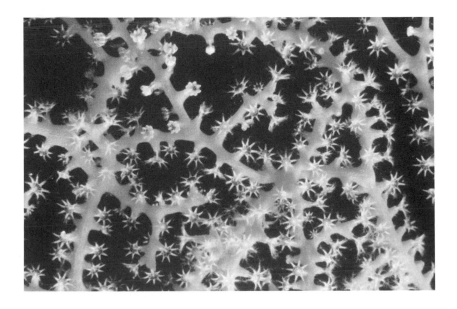

Fig. 3.4   *Gorgonians are colonial animals, each of which has eight tiny tentacles.* (Courtesy of Mohammed Al Momany, Aqaba, Jordan, NOAA)

includes some of the most unusual and colorful deep-sea organisms, including soft corals, sea fans, sea whips, and sea pens. Sea fans are not always shaped like fans; some look like bushes and others resemble bottlebrushes. The soft, golden coral in the upper color insert on page C-2 has a delicate structure.

Paragorgia arborea is a soft, deepwater octocoral. Forming fleshy, treelike shaped structures that can reach 10 feet (3 m) in height, *Paragorgia arborea* is the largest benthic invertebrate. Other families of gorgonians that are common in deep water of the Atlantic include Anthothelidae, Acanthogorgiidae, Paragorgiidae, Plexauridae, Ellisellidae, Primnoidae, Chrysogorgiidae and Isididae.

Hydrozoans are colonial cnidarians that may either be sessile or floating. Hydrozoans differ from anemones because their life cycles include both the polyp and medusa forms. In addition, the animals live as a colony, where they divide the labor and share a common gastrovascular cavity. Individual animals, or zooids, specialize, some in charge of capturing food, others taking care of tasks such as reproduction, staying afloat, and digesting food. All hydroids are carnivores that capture prey with stinging tentacles. Many of the sessile forms resemble small stalks or fuzzy balls of algae.

The floating hydrozoans, or siphonophores, have a gelatinous quality, so they superficially resemble jellyfish. However, each "individual" hydrozoan is actually composed of a group of as many as one thousand small animals or zooids. Many species of hydrozoans grow tentacles, some less than an inch (2.54 cm) long and others more than six feet (1.8 m) long. Most siphonophores bioluminesce when they move, emitting a soft, blue light. To avoid sinking, some possess swimming medusae; others rely on gas-filled floats, while a number have both medusae and floats.

One of the best-known and most-feared siphonophores is the bluebottle, or Portuguese man-of-war (*Physalia physalis*). Living on the surface of the water column, the Portuguese man-of-war has pale blue coloration. As in all hydrozoans, the individuals within the colony are highly specialized. Because *Physalia* lacks a bell-shaped medusa, like a true jellyfish, it depends on its pneumatophore, the gas-filled float, to hold the colony at the water's surface. Below the float are the zooids. The dactylozooids are individuals that have sticky nematocyst-armed tentacles. Growing up to six feet (1.8 m) long, dactylozooids capture food by dangling in the water waiting for prey. Living among the dactylozooids are the feeding zooids, called gastrozooids, and the gonozooids that produce eggs and sperm.

Other siphonophores, such as *Apalemia,* possess swimming medusae as well as gas-filled floats. Reaching lengths of 98 feet (30 m), *Apalemia* spread across the water, catching prey like a stinging fish net. The feeding and reproductive zooids of *Apalemia* are contained in a long, stemlike structure that trails behind the swimming zooids.

Muggiaea is a floating hydrozoan that has a medusa but lacks a gas-filled float. To swim, the bell pulses open and closed, shooting the animal forward and dragging the zooids behind it. To help the colony stay afloat, *Muggiaea* contains droplets of oil in the tips of its bell.

The deepwater hydrozoan *Solmissus* is an active and aggressive predator that feeds almost exclusively on jellyfish. Instead of pulling its tentacles behind a swimming bell, *Solmissus* swims with its tentacles thrust forward. This position enables the hydrozoan to reach out and grab prey.

Members of the class Scyphozoa are the true jellyfish. Most are small animals, about 3 inches (10 cm) wide, but a few grow up to 10 feet (3 m) with tentacles dangling up to 230 feet (70 m) into the water. Jellyfish, like the one in the lower color insert on page C-2, spend their entire lives in the medusa stage. All are carnivores that prey on zooplankton and small fish.

One deepwater jellyfish, *Atolla vanhoeffeni,* is abundant worldwide. Brightly colored with a red and purple medusa, the 1.2-inch (3-cm) animal emits a soft bioluminescent light when disturbed. Twenty short, stiff feeding tentacles extend from the bell along with one long tentacle, whose function is still unknown. *Atolla vanhoeffeni* is abundant at depths of 640 to 3,300 feet (500 to 1,000 m). A larger species, *Atolla wyvillei,* can be found as deep as 16,404 feet (5,000 m).

A jellyfish that lives in water more than 2,000 feet deep (610 m) is *Tiburonia granrojo*. Named *granrojo* after the Spanish word for "big red," this blood-red ball measures two to three feet (60 to 90 cm) wide. Most of this jellyfish's time is spent floating in cold, deep water, searching for prey. *Tiburonia granrojo* is an unusual species because it lacks tentacles. Several short, stumpy arms extend from this animal's bell and may be used in gathering food.

Ctenophores

Ctenophores, or comb jellies, are a small group of marine invertebrates that resemble jellyfish. They are not classified as cnidarians because they lack nematocysts. Comb jellies are named for the eight rows of comb plates on their radially symmetrical, translucent bodies. Although the comb plates are covered with short, hairlike cilia that are constantly in motion, the animals are only weak swimmers and are usually carried along by the energy of the water. Translucent and difficult to see in the daytime, comb jellies are bioluminescent at night. A bioluminescent comb jelly is shown in the upper color insert on page C-3.

In the open ocean, species grow large, some reaching lengths of 3.3 feet (1 m). Many of the surface-dwelling species, such as *Deiopea kaloktenota,* are transparent, but those that live deeper in the water column are pigmented. Tortugas red, a red comb jelly that lives in deep water, was only recently discovered and has not been assigned a scientific name. Like all comb jellies, Tortugas red is a carnivore that captures food with tentacles that are covered with specialized adhesive cells called colloblasts.

Worms

Every square inch of the deep ocean floor is populated with marine worms. Some are free-swimming, but most live in the substrate, feeding on detritus or preying on dead animals. Marine worms play an important role in breaking down organic matter, helping to convert detritus into carbon dioxide gas. Carbon dioxide rises to the surface where it is used in photosynthesis. Marine worms are also involved in the nitrogen cycle, making this valuable nutrient available to the food chain. A few species of worms survive by parasitizing other marine animals.

Worms are more complex than either sponges or cnidarians. Most worms can be classified into one of three major groups: flatworms (phylum Turbellaria), roundworms (phylum Nematoda), and segmented worms (phylum Annelida). All are bilaterally symmetrical, have three body layers, and display distinct anterior and posterior ends. Bilateral symmetry is an advancement over radial symmetry because it enables an animal to develop a streamlined shape and to group the majority of its sense organs at the anterior end, the part of the animal that first encounters new things in the environment.

Of the three groups, the flatworms are the simplest. As the name suggests, flatworms are thin and flat, lacking segments or appendages. Animals in the flatworm group range in size from a fraction of an inch to 20 inches (50 cm) in length. On the ventral side, a flatworm's epidermal layer is covered with cilia, enabling the worm to deposit a mucus trail along which it can glide.

A flatworm's anterior end is equipped with chemoreceptors, sense organs that help the organism find its food by detecting chemicals in the water. Once suitable food is located, a muscular, tubelike pharynx extends from the digestive system, pumps out digestive enzymes onto the meal, then sucks up partially digested tissue. Many flatworms are so translucent that their highly branched digestive tracts show through their skin. Wastes are expelled through the single opening in the digestive tract or they are excreted through the epidermis. The epidermis also serves as the site of gas exchange.

Flatworms may reproduce in several ways, depending on species. Some divide asexually by fission, producing two identical offspring. Other species have all-female populations whose eggs develop without fertilization. However, most types of flatworms reproduce sexually. Generally, individual flatworms are hermaphrodites, having both male and female reproductive organs. To cross-fertilize their gametes, two worms copulate, each donating sperm to the other.

Flukes and tapeworms are two types of parasitic flatworms. Flukes, which can be internal or external parasites, have complex life cycles that usually involve more than one host animal. Tapeworms, on the other hand, spend their entire lives within the digestive tract of one animal. The largest tapeworms, which can grow to lengths of 99 feet (30 m), live in the digestive tracts of sperm whales.

Nematodes, or roundworms, are much more numerous than flatworms. Most nematodes are just a fraction of an inch long and are thus invisible to the naked eye, but a few parasitic species are larger. Marine roundworms are the most abundant residents of marine sediments, living between the particles of soil where they feed on microscopic organisms and detritus.

The bodies of annelids, the segmented worms, are divided into distinct sections, an advance over the design of flatworms and roundworms. Segments enable worms to develop specialized body parts and to increase in length by adding more sections. Polychaetes, segmented worms with bristles, or *setae,* along their external surfaces, represent the largest group of marine annelids. Setae usually occur in bundles as part of the structure of the polychaete foot, or parapodium. In some worms, parapodia are tiny bumps, but in others they are prominent lobed appendages with gills and fingerlike projections. Generally, parapodia are more developed in swimming worms than in burrowing ones.

Sexes are separate in polychaetes. During reproduction, worms release sperm and eggs into the water where they unite to form zygotes. Zygotes grow into planktonic larvae that swim in the water for a short time. Eventually, they settle to the bottom and metamorphose into the adult forms.

Some species of polychaetes are free-living while others have sedentary lifestyles. The free-living, or errant, worms actively search for food. The body of an errant species is long and slender and looks about the same from head to tail. Errant worms are predators, and the head-end is equipped with jaws and teeth. Sedentary polychaetes are shorter and have three distinct body sections. Instead of preying on other animals, they are either filter feeders or deposit feeders, which collect detritus. Some sedentary polychaetes live in tubes that they build from grains of sediment, mucus, calcium carbonate, or a paperlike protein.

Polychaetes are found in abundance around cold-water coral banks, geothermal vents, and the bodies of dead ocean animals. Because exploring the deep seafloor is a relatively new venture, many of these worms have only recently been discovered. When scientists visited several whale carcasses on the deep seafloor, they found polychaete worms so abundant at the sites that the mass of their bodies looked like thick shag carpet. These short, centipedelike worms are new to science and have not yet been named.

Research at geothermal vents turned up the largest polychaete ever found, the deep sea tubeworms, or vent worm (*Riftia pachyptila*). *Riftia* specimens have been discovered that are 10 feet (3 m) long and two to three inches (5 to 8 cm) wide. Shown in Figure 3.5, giant tubeworms are unusual in that they lack both a mouth and a digestive system. For nutrition, *Riftia* are completely dependent on the presence of symbiotic bacteria in their tissues. Within a worm, bacteria live inside a structure called a trophosome.

Riftia live in white tubes made out of a tough material called chitin. The posterior ends of tubes are anchored to the seafloor, and the anterior ends, surrounded by rings of blood-red tentacles, wave in the water column. These tentacles are the site of gas exchange. Their red coloration is due to the presence of a blood molecule, hemoglobin, that can bind to oxygen and hydrogen sulfide, two critically important gases in the geothermal vent community. The circulatory system in the worms delivers the oxygen to body tissues and takes the hydrogen sulfide to the bacteria in the trophosome; there, the bacteria oxidize hydrogen sulfide and use the energy that results from that oxidation to make food. Some of the food produced by each bacterium leaks out into tissues of the host worm and provides its nutrition. In this symbiotic relationship, the worms and bacteria are completely dependent on one another: The bacteria make food for the worm, and the worm

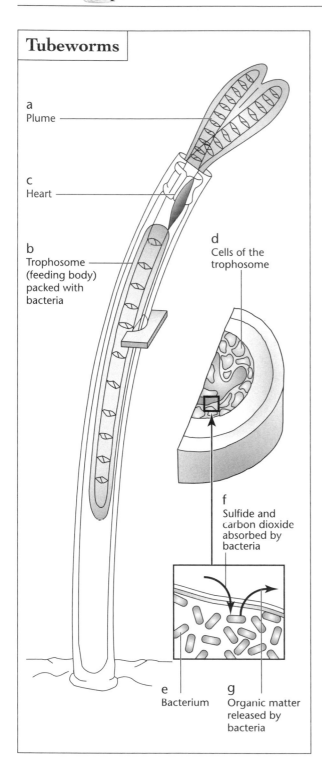

Tubeworms

a
Plume

c
Heart

b
Trophosome
(feeding body)
packed with
bacteria

d
Cells of the
trophosome

f
Sulfide and
carbon dioxide
absorbed by
bacteria

e
Bacterium

g
Organic matter
released by
bacteria

collects hydrogen sulfide for the bacteria and protects them from predators.

For most animals, hydrogen sulfide is toxic, yet *Riftia* gathers the material for its chemosynthetic bacteria without suffering any ill effects. The ability of hemoglobin to bind hydrogen sulfide very closely keeps the poison away from the worm's other tissues. The circulatory system of *Riftia* carries the hydrogen sulfide straight to the bacteria, which take it up and use it immediately.

Vent communities are relatively short-lived, sometimes collapsing after just a few decades of development, and the seafloor is dotted with old vent mounds. For this reason, animals that live around geothermal vents mature rapidly. Vent worms are the fastest-growing of all invertebrates. No one is sure how the worms initially find newly formed geothermal vents, but scientists do know that populations of the animals appear quickly and start

Fig. 3.5   Giant tubeworms (Riftia pachyptila) *lack mouths and digestive systems. The top of the worm is the plume (a), where the worm picks up oxygen and hydrogen sulfide. Bacteria live in a special organ, the trophosome (b). A muscular heart (c) pumps blood from the plume to the trophosome and other body structures. Cells in the trophosome (d) contain bacteria (e). Hydrogen sulfide and carbon dioxide (f) are absorbed by the bacteria, which use the gases to make food. Food in the form of organic compounds is released by the bacteria (g) and taken up by the worm for nutrition.*

new colonies. Research on geothermal vent communities shows that the worms reproduce by spawning, releasing their eggs and sperm into the water.

Arrowworms are a small group of organisms made up of only 150 species found in the open ocean as well as in the deep sea. The transparent, dart-shaped worms range in size from 0.12 to 4.7 inches (3 mm to 12 cm). They have fins for swimming and stabilizing their position in water, a pair of hooked spines on each side of the head for grasping prey, and several spines that hang down around their heads. When an arrow worm swims, a hood covers these spines, perhaps an adaptation to reduce drag in the water. In some respects, arrowworms are similar to roundworms in that they lack respiratory, circulatory, and excretory body systems. However, their mouths contain teeth, and they have compound eyes and nervous systems. Despite their delicate size and appearance, arrowworms are voracious predators that consume as much as 37 percent of their body weight a day. They feed on small, insectlike animals in the zooplankton and other worms.

Conclusion

Life in the open and deep sea has traditionally been difficult to study. Since the technology to study deep water has only been available for the last 20 years, much of the current knowledge is still new and speculative. In many ways scientists have been surprised at the environmental challenges that animals face in these poorly understood parts of the ocean. Open-water invertebrates must survive in nutrient-poor waters where supplies of food are patchy and protection is nonexistent. Deep-sea animals deal with total darkness, cold temperatures, high pressure, and scarce food.

Despite these difficult living conditions, sponges are highly successful deep-sea, benthic organisms. Essentially unchanged from their ancestral forms, sponges are the simplest animals. These filter feeders depend on the movement of water through their asymmetrical bodies for nutrition. Scientists divide sponges into groups based on the types of spicules found in their bodies. The glass sponges, which are supported by spicules made of silica, are dominant deep-sea species. They form important reef structures and therefore provide habitats for a variety of other kinds of deepwater animals.

Cnidarians are more complex than sponges because they have simple, one-way digestive systems. All cnidarians share common characteristics such as tentacles, nematocysts, and gastrovascular cavities. Three subgroups of cnidarians are anthozoans, hydrozoans, and scyphozoans. The anthozoans are sessile animals that include corals such as *Lophelia* and *Oculina*. *Lophelia* is the dominant coral in the Darwin Mounds, cold-water reefs found in the northeastern section of the Atlantic Ocean. The hydrozoans, colonial cnidarians, include the Portuguese man-of-war, a blue-colored collection of zooids that lives at the surface of the water. Within the colony, individual zooids are specialized to carry out specific jobs to support the group.

True jellyfish, the scyphozoans spend their lives as weakly swimming medusae. Jellyfish can be found from the top of the water column to the very deep regions of the bathyal zone. Unlike the jellylike colonies of hydrozoans, a jellyfish is just one animal. Found in the deep water, a new species has recently been named *Tiburonia granrojo*, a tribute to its bright-red color. Ctenophores, or comb jellies, are similar to jellyfish but are distinguished by their lack of nematocysts.

Three large groups of worms—flatworms, roundworms, and segmented worms—are important parts of the benthic ecosystem. Another, much smaller group, commonly known as arrowworms, preys on plankton. Flatworms, the simplest worms, may be free-living or parasitic. Segmented worms, the most advanced group, show evolutionary advances that are reflected in mollusks, arthropods, and echinoderms, more advanced invertebrates.

4

Mollusks, Crustaceans, and Echinoderms
Advanced Invertebrates of the Open Ocean

*I*nvertebrates live throughout the open ocean, from the sunlit surface waters to trenches that reach depths of almost seven miles (11.3 km). Within this vast area there are hundreds of unique environments, each inhabited by a particular group of animals. The warm, uppermost waters, for example, are perfect homes for billions of tiny, insectlike animals that feed on phytoplankton. In the deep sea, sea cucumbers burrow through silty bottoms, octopuses hide among deepwater corals, and sponges grow on the sides of seamounts. Even similar habitats in different parts of the marine world yield unique combinations of animals. In the Atlantic Ocean, geothermal vents support eyeless shrimp in populations that are so dense they appear to be solid, living walls. In the Pacific Ocean, clams, mussels, and giant worms dominate vent communities.

Most animals that live in the deep sea are smaller than their relatives near the surface or in shallow water. The difference in their sizes may be due to the overall scantiness of food in deep water. On the other hand, a few types of deepwater organisms grow to gigantic size. Deep-sea gigantism is a difficult phenomenon for scientists to explain, and no one knows for sure why it occurs.

Mollusks, arthropods, and echinoderms are invertebrates that have well-developed body systems for taking care of functions such as digestion, coordination, reproduction, and respiration. Within the respiratory system, specialized organs called *gills* extract dissolved oxygen from water. Gills are made of thin, highly folded tissues that are packed with tiny blood vessels. As water flows over gills, oxygen in the water diffuses directly into the blood stream, while carbon dioxide in the blood diffuses out into the water. Blood is the component of the circulatory system that binds to oxygen and delivers it to all cells. The circulatory system also plays a role in transporting nutrient molecules produced by the digestive system to cells and collecting cellular wastes for delivery to the excretory system. All of these body systems are interdependent and are run and coordinated by the nervous system, which is usually centralized at the anterior end of the animal.

Invertebrates living in deep-sea habitats are similar to species that inhabit shallow water but exhibit special adaptations for their unique environments. To cope with the extremely high water pressure, the bodies of animals do not have any air spaces in their tissues like their shallow-water relatives. All of the tissue spaces of deepwater animals are filled with fluids, a modification that enables the animals to maintain their shape and structure. Other adaptations include enlarged gills, a structural adaptation to help animals get as much oxygen as possible out of relatively low-oxygen environments, and modified eyes for life in total darkness.

Mollusks

No matter what part of the ocean one explores, mollusks can be found there. Mollusks are a large group of organisms with more than 50,000 species, making them second in number only to the arthropods. Even though they show a remarkable diversity in size and shape, mollusks share several common characteristics: a mantle, a muscular foot, and a tonguelike feeding organ.

The mollusk body is covered with a thin tissue called the *mantle.* In some species the mantle secretes the shell and one or more defensive chemicals, like ink, mucus, or acid. Most mollusks have a foot, a muscular organ that can be used for locomotion, whether it be swimming, digging, or crawling. In addition, all mollusks, except for the bivalves, feed by scraping up food with a *radula,* a muscular, filelike organ. The bivalves are filter feeders that trap and consume food particles suspended in water.

In mollusks, sexes are separate. Bivalves release their eggs and sperm into the water, and fertilization occurs there. In other types of mollusks, sperm are transferred into the body of the female and fertilization occurs internally. The female deposits strings, or cases, of eggs on soil or rocks. In both internal and external fertilization, zygotes develop into swimming larvae that metamorphose into adult forms.

The shells of mollusks are their most noticeable features. Shells are designed to protect the animal's soft body parts. The presence or absence of a shell is one of several characteristics used to divide mollusks into subgroups: gastropods, snails, slugs, and their relatives; bivalves, a group that includes clams and mussels; and cephalopods such as squid and octopuses.

Gastropods

The term *gastropod* literally means "stomach foot" and refers to the muscular foot that extends from the stomach area of the animals' bodies. The foot can be used as a method of locomotion or to secure the animal to a firm substrate. Most gastropods have a shell, although a few species do not. In some species, an *operculum*, a flap or door that can close the shell, protects the occupant from danger. The head of a gastropod is equipped with sensory organs including light-sensitive dots, tentacles, and a mouth.

In shallow water, gastropods may be herbivores, carnivores, or detritivores. In deep water, the majority of benthic gastropods scavenge food. Since food is scarce in the deep ocean, even scavenging becomes highly specialized. For example, one kind of mollusk dines exclusively on the hard, hornlike beaks of dead octopuses and squid, while another type specializes in the empty egg cases of sharks and rays. Some of the gastropods, including *Cataegis finkli*, a snail with an elaborately swirled shell, feed on the dead pieces of sea grasses and macroalgae that drift to the seafloor. *Bathybembix* is a small snail that feeds on organic matter that accumulates in sediment.

Despite the preponderance of scavengers, a few mollusks exhibit alternative feeding styles. Turrids, animals that are close relatives of the shallow-water cone shells, are predators that dine on worms living in the sediment. To kill their prey, these gastropods inject them with venom through the teeth on their radulae. Members of a group of small snails in the family

Eulimidae parasitize sea stars in deep water by permanently attaching to their hosts and sucking out their body fluids.

On the surface of the open ocean, a small group of uncharacteristic gastropods has been very successful. The pteropods either lack, or have a reduced, shell. Large sections of the pteropod foot are broadened into winglike shapes. This unusual anatomy makes it possible for pteropods to swim near the water's surface.

The naked sea butterfly (*Clione limacine*), so called because it lacks a shell, is a pteropod whose transparent body is streaked with shades of pink, orange, and yellow. At night, pteropods swim at the surface and feed on phytoplankton. During the day, when they are most likely to be spotted by predators, sea butterflies move to deeper waters. Like most pteropods, sea butterflies are hermaphrodites. To reproduce, two animals intertwine their bodies and exchange sperm.

Another group of gastropods with atypical bodies are heteropods. Preferring warm water, heteropods are most often found in open seas of temperate and tropical zones. The gastropod foot of a heteropod is modified to form one or two fins, depending on the species, which the animal uses for swimming. A heteropod is an active swimmer and an aggressive predator that relies on its well-developed eyes to spot prey. In some species, sexes are separate, but in others the adult animals are hermaphrodites. In a few cases, all animals begin life as males, then convert to females as they age. After fertilization, eggs are released into the water column in long strings that drift until they hatch.

Bivalves

Bivalves are mollusks whose soft body parts are covered by two shells, or valves, that hinge on one side. The shells are held together by strong adductor muscles that attach to their inside surfaces. Clams and mussels are two types of bivalves found in deep water.

To move, a bivalve extends its foot through partially opened shells. Depending on the species, locomotion may involve swimming, crawling, or burrowing in the sediment. As shown in Figure 4.1, burrowing bivalves also possess two siphons, tubes that transport water to and from the gills that are located in the mantle cavity. In filter-feeding bivalves, gills have the additional function of gathering food. Mucus on the gills traps particles that are suspended in the water, then the cilia move the food to the mouth.

The majority of clams are filter feeders, but one group of deep-sea clams is carnivorous. In these organisms, the gill filaments are modified so that the clams can pull water in quickly, trapping tiny copepods and amphipods. Cilia move the trapped prey to the clam's mouth.

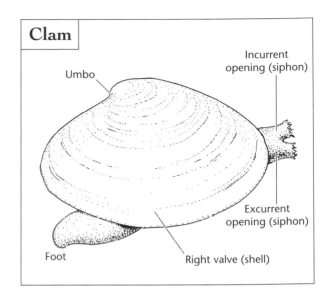

Fig. 4.1 A clam is a mollusk whose body is protected by two valves and equipped with a muscular foot for locomotion.

Some of the most successful bivalves in geothermal vent communities are those that develop symbiotic relationships with sulfur bacteria. Giant clams (*Calyptogena magnifica*), like the specimens shown in the lower color insert on page C-3, live on the slopes of vent chimneys. The animals are appropriately named since adults may grow to one foot (27 cm) in length. Unlike typical bivalves, giant clams lack mouths and digestive systems and depend on sulfur bacteria within their bodies to make their food.

Giant clams and sulfur bacteria have a nearly perfect symbiotic arrangement. The blood of giant clams contains hemoglobin, which helps bind oxygen and transport it to all the cells. Hemoglobin also binds hydrogen sulfide and delivers it to the sulfur bacteria living on the bivalves' gills, which are enlarged to accommodate these symbionts. Energy harvested from the breakdown of hydrogen sulfide is used to assemble carbon atoms into food molecules. The carbon needed to make food comes from the clam's respiration. Some of the food manufactured by the bacteria leaks out of the bacterial cells and into the tissues of the clams, nourishing them.

A bivalve living alongside a deep-sea vent must keep its body within a very narrow zone of water. To do so, the bivalve wedges its muscular foot between rocks on the seafloor and continually adjusts its position. Ideally the animal can get close enough to the vent to take in water that is rich in hydrogen sulfide but remain out of water that is hot enough to damage tissues.

Cephalopods

Cephalopods, or the "head-foot" animals, have their locomotive structures, arms, located near their heads. All are accomplished predators that use both arms and tentacles to snare prey. Once prey is subdued, it is pushed into the cephalopods' beaklike mouths, which are well designed for killing and tearing off tissue.

One of a cephalopod's most distinguishing characteristics is its advanced nervous system. Cephalopods have the largest brains of any invertebrates, enabling them to process information and learn new things. Much of the information coming into the cephalopod brain arrives through well-developed eyes. Another source of information is the tentacles, which are sensitive touch receptors and capable of distinguishing chemicals in the water.

There are three major groups of cephalopods: octopuses, squid, and cuttlefish. The body of an octopus is made up of a mantle, a head, and eight arms, each of which has one or two rows of suckers. A squid has a mantle, a head, eight arms, two tentacles, and two fins. Both the arms and tentacles are covered with suckers. A cuttlefish has a head, a mantle, eight arms, two tentacles, and two fins. Squid and cuttlefish are active, swimming predators, while octopuses creep up on slower, benthic prey.

Octopuses lack bones or shells, internally and externally. Squid and cuttlefish have oval, flattened internal bones that give their bodies structural support and provide a point of attachment for muscles. The bone of a cuttlefish is porous and capable of holding gas. Cuttlefish can adjust the amount of gas in this bone, thus regulating their position in the water. The internal bone of squid is a nonporous, gelatinous rod called the gladius.

As a general rule, octopuses are small animals, measuring less than 11.8 inches (30 cm) in diameter. Most are solitary hunters crawling across the seafloor when searching for food. If startled or threatened, the octopus may use its jet-propulsion system to escape, sucking water into a muscular sac located in the mantle cavity, then forcefully expelling it out a narrow siphon. Many octopuses build dens where they rest during the day and where females lay and protect their eggs.

In the summer of 2000 an extensive, deep-sea octopus nursery was located by scientists doing research on the Gorda Escarpment, a plateau 100 miles (161 km) off the coast of California and one mile (1,600 m) below the water's surface. It was not until July of 2002 that funding was available for scientists to return to the area and evaluate their earlier find. Researchers saw thousands of octopuses curled around clutches of eggs. Even though it is not unusual for a female octopus to *brood*, or watch over, her eggs, scientists had never witnessed so many animals in one place. In addition, an equal number of small fish were also brooding eggs. Scientists speculate that this particular escarpment is a popular nesting site because of its location. Rocks, which provide good places to lay eggs, are strewn across the seafloor and a strong oxygen- and food-laden current flows over the region. Two of the most common types of octopus at the Gorda Escarpment are *Graneledone* and *Benthoctopus*.

Squid are also found in the deep part of the ocean, either in small schools or as solitary individuals. Squid have a unique adaptation for maintaining their buoyancy in seawater. Pockets of tissue in the squid's body hold an ammonia solution that is manufactured from the squid's own urine. Since ammonia is less dense than water, these pockets act like floats.

The vampire squid (*Vampyroteuthis infernalis*), shown in the photo, is an atypical species that lives in very deep water. Measuring only about eight inches (20 cm) long, this black or red animal is neither a vampire nor a true squid. Instead, the vampire squid shows traits of both squid and octopuses. The eight arms of this animal are webbed, and it has two long sensory filaments that can be retracted and stored in pouches near the eyes. The sensory filaments help locate prey, usually small fish. The arms of vampire squid, which are covered with sharp, toothlike projections, are used for defense and to subdue prey.

All types of squid have fins on the sides of their body, but the two large fins of vampire squid are positioned in such a way that they superficially resemble ears. This deepwater squid has extremely big eyes, the largest of any animal its size. Most squid and octopuses have rough skin, but the body of the vampire squid has a gelatinous texture. The lower part of the body and the arms are covered with light-producing organs called photophores

Even the part of the ocean where this animal lives is unusual. The vampire squid is at home in the part of the deepwater column called the oxygen minimum zone (OMZ), an area that scientists have traditionally considered too low in oxygen to support living things that require the gas for their metabolism. The vampire squid can survive in the OMZ because its gills have an enormous surface area, making them super-efficient at gathering oxygen from water. In addition, the blood of a vampire squid contains a molecule called hemocyanin, which very efficiently binds to oxygen. Hemocyanin also colors the blood blue.

Another unique species of squid can be found in the midwater column of the open ocean. The wonky-eyed jewel squid has an enlarged left eye and a normal-size right eye. This species uses its enlarged eye to look for prey, while the smaller one faces straight down in the water to watch for predators. The body of the wonky-eyed jewel squid is partially covered with small, iridescent spots that emit a soft, jewel-like light. The faint light produced by these spots is directed downward in the water and has the effect of eliminating the animal's silhouette against the surface. Depending on the time of day and the amount of light filtering through the water, the squid can adjust the brightness of its spots.

The giant squid (*Architeutis dux*), the largest of all invertebrates, lives in the deep parts of the ocean, at depths of 660 to 2,300 feet (200 to 700 m). Research on the giant squid is incomplete because very few specimens have been available for study. Scientists know that the average length of an adult female giant squid, the larger of the sexes, is 60 feet (18 m) from the tip of the body to the tip of the longest tentacle. Each eye of the giant squid measures over one foot (30 cm) in diameter. The squid's arms are equipped with hundreds of suction cups, each one held up on a stalk and armed with a ring of sharp teeth that pierce prey as the cups clasp it tightly. The carcasses of giant squids have washed up on coasts of Norway, New Zealand, the United Kingdom, and the United States. Such a wide distribution of animals suggests that the squids live in deep waters worldwide.

Modern cephalopods developed from ancestral forms that had shells. Only two species of shelled cephalopods still exist. The shells of species belonging to the genus *Nautilus* are made up of many individual chambers, each containing gas. The nautilus migrates vertically in the open ocean by adjusting the amount of gas in its shell. The daylight hours are spent at depths of 1,800 feet (548.6 m), but at night the animals travel up in the water column to feed. *Nautilus* species can be found in the South Pacific and Indian Oceans.

Arthropods

Arthropods are a large group of animals on land and in the sea. Terrestrial arthropods include insects and spiders, and familiar marine species are shrimp and crabs. An arthropod's body is

Advantages and Disadvantages of an Exoskeleton

More than 80 percent of the animal species are equipped with a hard, outer covering called an exoskeleton. The functions of exoskeletons are similar to those of other types of skeletal systems. Like the internal skeletons (endoskeletons) of amphibians, reptiles, birds, and mammals, exoskeletons support the tissues and give shape to the bodies of invertebrates. Exoskeletons offer some other advantages. Serving as a suit of armor, they are excellent protection against predators. Also, because they completely cover an animal's tissues, exoskeletons prevent them from drying out. In addi-tion, exoskeletons serve as points of attachment for muscles, providing animals with more leverage and mechanical advantage than an endoskeleton can offer. That is why a tiny shrimp can cut a fish in half with its claw or lift an object 50 times heavier than its own body.

Despite all their good points, exoskeletons have some drawbacks. They are heavy, so the only animals that have been successful with them over time are those that have remained small. In addi-tion, an animal must molt, or shed, its exoskeleton to grow. During and imme-diately after a molt, an animal is unpro-tected and vulnerable to predators.

divided into segments to which several types of appendages are attached. An appendage is a leg, antenna, or other part that extends from a segment of the body. An exoskeleton protects the body and its vulnerable internal organs.

In most arthropods, sexes are separate. In many species the male deposits sperm in the female's body, where they remain until the eggs leave the ovary. Zygotes that result from the fusion of egg and sperm mature into larvae that settle to the seafloor to mature.

Crustaceans

The largest division of arthropods is the crustaceans, a group that includes crabs, shrimp, and lobsters. Crustaceans have three specialized body sections: head, thorax, and abdomen. The head is equipped with two sets of antennae and three sets of feeding appendages. In some species, one set of feeding appendages end in claws that are large and capable of exerting hundreds of pounds of pressure. The body and abdomen of a crustacean possesses walking or swimming appendages. Sexually, the animals have separate genders, and females are in charge of egg-laying and brooding.

Small crustaceans like copepods are some of the most common members of zooplankton. Most are herbivorous animals that eat half their weight in phytoplankton every day. *Calanus pacificus,* a typical oceanic copepod, has antennae longer than its bullet-shaped body. To swim, the animal pulls its antennae down and back like the oars of a rowboat, shooting forward in jerky strokes.

At night, *Calanus pacificus* feeds on phytoplankton in the upper regions of the water column. During the day, it swims into deeper water to avoid predators. This daily movement of hiding in deep water and returning to the surface to feed is described as diurnal migration.

Copepods have the distinction of being the fastest animals on Earth. When dodging their predators, copepods easily outpace cheetahs and racehorses. Copepods can propel their bodies through the water at speeds of 500 body lengths per second. To put this in perspective, an F-16 jet fighter moves at 50 body lengths per second!

Euphausiids, or krill, featured in the upper color insert on page C-4, are one- to two-inch-long (3 to 6 cm) crustaceans that play key roles in the open-ocean food chains of the Antarctic. *Euphausia pacifica* is the primary source of food for fish, sea birds, and marine mammals. At times, *Euphausia pacifica* occur in dense aggregations that attract predators of all types. Most species of *Euphausia* are bioluminescent, producing their light in structures called photophores. Scientists speculate that the light may be used to help draw individuals together in swarms or to find a mate. In the Antarctic, billions of *Euphausia superba* form swarms that cover hundreds of square yards of the sea's surface.

Marine isopods are small crustaceans that resemble their terrestrial relatives, the pill bugs and sow bugs. Most range in length from 0.12 to 0.39 inches (3 to 10 mm) and have common names such as sea lice, fish lice, tongue-biter, and sea centipedes. Small isopods are often parasites on fish and marine mammals. Paradoxically, one of the largest of all crustaceans is

Krill

Despite its frigid temperatures, the Southern Ocean near Antarctica is teeming with life. The food web there is supported by diatoms, which are nourished by upwelling currents that carry nutrients from deep seafloors to surface water. Diatoms provide food for many species of zooplankton, the most numerous of which are tiny crustaceans called krill. Krill, shown in the upper color insert on page C-4, are shrimplike creatures that range from one to two inches (3 to 6 cm) in length.

On the zooplankton scale, krill are large animals whose weight makes it difficult to stay afloat. To prevent sinking, krill swim constantly. Because swimming expends a lot of energy these crustaceans require a tremendous amount of food. To meet this need, krill feed constantly, collecting diatoms by pumping water through net-like combs on their legs.

In the summer, when warm temperatures and long days boost the size of diatom populations, populations of krill soar. In some areas, swarms of krill cover hundreds of meters of sea surface. In the winter, productivity drops to almost zero because of short days and cold temperatures. During this period, krill live in deeper waters and feed on detritus.

Krill are important sources of food for a variety of continental shelf water animals. When productivity is high, whales, birds, fish, squid, and hundreds of other types of organisms travel to the southern waters to feed. Scientists estimate that during a typical summer, fish consume more than 100 million tons of the tiny crustaceans. A blue whale can take in a ton of krill at each feeding, and most blue whales feed four times a day. Krill also makes up almost 80 percent of the diet of seabirds in the region.

a free-living isopod, *Bathynomus giganteus*. Found on the seafloor of very deep water, this species grows to about a half yard (1/2 m) long.

Shrimp and crabs are deep- and open-ocean crustaceans whose first pair of legs are claws. Shrimp, the smaller of the two, have relatively lightweight exoskeletons and gills located under their shells. Most shrimp begin life as males and then change into females during midlife. After fertilization, developing eggs cling to the female's swimming legs, where they remain until they hatch. Shrimp larvae swim freely for two or three months before settling into the mature shrimp lifestyle in the water column or on the seafloor.

Shrimp are found throughout the ocean, even near the deepwater hydrothermal vents. In the Atlantic Ocean, vent shrimp (*Rimicaris exoculata*) are extremely abundant. Vent shrimp have no eyes, an adaptation to total darkness that is not too surprising to marine biologists. The discovery of light-sensitive patches of tissues on the dorsal surfaces of these animals has put scientists in a quandary. The patch of tissue, made up of the same pigments found in the eyes of animals, cannot see images but can detect light.

Discovering light-sensitive shrimp in a pitch-black environment spurred scientists to investigate the area for any sources of light. Experiments showed that the vents themselves emit infrared, or heat, light. The shrimp may detect this light and use it as a beacon to help them position their bodies close to the vents. Visits to deep-sea vents in submersibles have shown that the shrimp live in swarms near the vent structures, hovering in groups as dense as 30,000 animals per 1.2 square yards (30,000 animals per m^2). By remaining near the vents, their bodies are constantly surrounded by water that contains hydrogen sulfide. As a result, sulfur bacteria grow on their bodies and antennae, coating their surfaces. When the populations of sulfur bacteria reach optimal size, the shrimp scrap them off and eat them.

Crabs, like the one shown crawling over tube worms and mussels in the lower color insert on page C-4, are residents of the seafloor at all depths, including the area around geothermal vents. King crabs are deep-sea residents whose long legs enable them to easily stride across the seafloor in search of prey. Like hermit crabs, their close relatives, the abdomens of king crabs are twisted to one side, and their legs fold in a way that enable them to walk forward, not just sideways like most shallow-water crabs. The extremely large eggs of king crabs produce shrimplike larvae. Instead of swimming in the plankton to look for food like other species of crabs, the larvae of king crabs do not eat but live off of stored yolk. This strategy may be an adaptation to living in water that is too far from the planktonic surface to incorporate a plankton-swimming developmental phase.

Squat lobsters, or galatheid crabs, are relatives of king crabs. *Munidopsis albatrossae* is a species that lives below 6,561.7 feet

(2,000 m) in habitats where there are corals, sponges, or rocks to hide in, such as the *Lophelia* coral reefs on the continental slopes of the eastern United States. Like many deep-sea animals, galatheid crabs are blind, since there is no light at this depth and eyes are not very helpful. Squat lobsters depend on their sense of smell to help them find food.

The body of the large-clawed spider crab (*Macroregonia macrochiera*) is 3.9 inches (10 cm) across, but its legs reach 19.7 inches (50 cm). The claw section of each front leg is over one foot (31 cm) long, giving these thin, long-legged crustaceans a resemblance to daddy longlegs spiders. Living in dark waters that are over 11,000 feet (3,400 m) deep in the Gulf of Alaska and other sites, large-clawed spider crabs have functional eyes, but scientists do not know why. One theory suggests that the eyes may be helpful in detecting bioluminescent light given off by organisms that congregate at foodfalls, places where the carcasses of dead animals fall to the seafloor. By following the light of glowing scavengers to such sites, the large-clawed spider crab can find a meal in an environment where food is extremely scarce. Once the crab feeds, it can go for a long time before it has to eat again.

Sea Spiders

Sea spiders are relatives of crabs and members of a primitive group of arthropods called chelicerates. All chelicerates lack antennae and jaws but have a tubular proboscis with which they pierce the body of a soft invertebrate and suck out the liquid portions. Terrestrial chelicerates include ticks, spiders, and scorpions. Sea spiders differ from their terrestrial cousins and namesakes in several ways. Unlike true spiders, whose bodies are made of two segments, sea spiders have three distinct body parts. In addition, sea spiders do not spin webs, and they have from four to six pairs of legs instead of four pairs.

Most sea spiders are extremely small, measuring only one-sixteenth of an inch (2 mm) in length. The female lays eggs that are externally fertilized by the male, the smaller of the pair. After fertilization, the male glues the eggs to his legs to protect them until they hatch into larvae. In some species, larvae are free-living, but in others they are parasites of cnidarians. By attaching to the medusae of free-living cnidarians, larvae are dispersed all over the ocean.

Echinoderms

Echinoderms, a group of spiny-skinned animals that include sea stars, sea cucumbers, sand dollars, and sea urchins, are widespread on the deep seafloor. The spiny skin characteristic of this group results from spikes of calcium carbonate that extend through the dorsal surface. At the base of the spines, tiny pincers called pedicellariae keep the body free of debris and parasites.

All echinoderms are radially symmetrical, and most have five or more arms extending from a central disk. The mouth of a sea star or a brittle star is located on the ventral surface in the center of the body, and the anus is on the dorsal surface, as indicated in Figure 4.3. In the deep sea, most echinoderms are predators or detritivores.

Fig. 4.3   On its ventral side, a sea star has a centrally located mouth surrounded by five arms that are covered with tube feet. The anus is located on the dorsal side; the skin on the dorsal side is covered with spines. (Courtesy of Dr. James P. McVey, NOAA Sea Grant Program)

The arms and central disk of an echinoderm are covered with tiny tube feet that act like suction cups. The suction cups are operated by a system of tubes that carry water. As the tube "feet" press against an object, water is withdrawn, creating suction. When water is returned to the cups, the suction is broken and the tube feet release their grip.

To reproduce, echinoderms release sperm and eggs that result in larvae. Larvae are free-swimming for a time before settling to the bottom and taking on typical adult echinoderm features. Most echinoderms can also reproduce asexually. If part of an animal breaks off, it may grow into a complete new organism. All are capable of regenerating missing body parts such as limbs, spines, and intestines.

Sea stars have five to 40 arms radiating from a central disk. Many are predators that will eat any small fish or invertebrate they can catch. One of the favorite foods of a sea star is a bivalve like a mussel. To open tightly closed mussel shells, the sea star pulls them apart with its tube feet, then pushes its own stomach between the shells, on top of the bivalve's soft body parts. Digestive juices in the sea star's stomach dissolve the mussel tissue, which the stomach then absorbs. Many types of sea stars live on the deep-sea floor, including a group known as slime stars.

Found at all depths of the ocean, brittle stars are small, thin echinoderms that use their flexible arms for swimming. Brittle stars get their names from the ease with which their arms break off if caught by a predator. Like all echinoderms, brittle stars are able to regenerate lost body parts and can regrow a damaged arm in a short time. Most species feed on detritus and microscopic organisms on the seafloor. Dominant deepwater brittle stars are *Ophiomusium glabrum*, *Amphiura carchara*, and *Amphilepis platytata*.

Sea urchins are echinoderms with long spines. Like sea stars, urchins move about the seafloor on tube feet. The fragile pink sea urchin (*Allocentrotus fragilis*) lives on the deep seafloor, rasping off bites of kelp that drift down from waters overhead with its five teeth. When food is not available, the pink sea urchin can live on its stores of fat.

Sea cucumbers are one of the dominant animals on the deep seafloor. One of the common deep-sea species is *Pannychia moseleyi*. All sea cucumbers are longer from mouth to anus than other kinds of echinoderms, giving them a wormlike appearance. Most species are small, only about 7.9 inches (20 cm) long, although one species (*Synapta maculate*) grows to lengths of 16.4 feet (5 m). To crawl, a sea cucumber contracts muscles in its leathery body or inches forward on ventral tube feet. Around the mouth several tube feet are modified to form tentacles. In some species tentacles strain suspended matter from the water, but others use them to shovel sand into their mouths so they can digest the organic matter in it.

Reproduction in sea cucumbers is sexual. Triggered by chemical signals, all of the sea cucumbers in an area simultaneously raise their bodies into cobralike positions, then release eggs and sperm. Gametes combine in the water to yield fertilized eggs, which grow into free-swimming larvae. Larvae eventually settle onto the seafloor and develop into adult sea cucumbers.

If a sea cucumber is threatened, it may eject tubules or bits of its intestines on an intruder. The sticky entrails confuse the intruder and give the sea cucumber a chance to escape. The sea cucumber can regenerate its lost organs.

Sea cucumbers can also be found in the sargassum beds of the Atlantic Ocean. The pink sea cucumber (*Opheodesoma spectabilis*) occurs in aggregates of 300 to 1,000 animals, feeding on the detritus of dead sargassum fronds with its retractable tentacles. To swim, the animal undulates its body through the water. Pink sea cucumbers can grow to lengths of 3.3 feet (1 m).

Crinoids, a group of echinoderms that include feather stars and sea lillies, are stalked animals. Although not a dominant factor on the seafloor today, the abundance of crinoid fossils suggests that the animals were more plentiful in the past. Like the ones shown attached to a dead sponge in the upper color insert on page C-5, crinoids feed by spreading their feathery arms and filtering food particles out of the water. Each crinoid arm is equipped with a groove that is bordered by tiny tube feet. Crinoids catch passing food particles with specialized terminal tube feet, then flick them into the groove. Mucus secreted by tube feet coat the food particle with mucus, and cilia sweep the food to the mouth.

Crinoids often live in groups, and several thousand individuals may be found together. Many are commensal with shrimp, crab, and brittle stars. Most crinoids are stationary but feather stars are capable of moving and will crawl from one location to another in search of food. During the day, feather stars may hide among rocks, but at night they stand upright and collect food.

Conclusion

Mollusks, arthropods, and echinoderms are complex invertebrates that can be found living in the open and deep oceans. All three types of animals have well-developed organ systems to handle functions such as digestion, respiration, reproduction, and excretion. Feeding styles vary from predation to scavenging dead organic matter.

Mollusks, which are characterized by a muscular foot, a mantle, and a radula, can be classified into three large groups: gastropods, bivalves, and cephalopods. In gastropods, the muscular foot is located near their stomachs or visceral organs. The foot can be used for locomotion or to attach the animal to a solid substrate. Snails and their relatives are gastropods that have one shell. A shell-less gastropod, the sea butterfly, lives in the upper part of the open-ocean water column.

Bivalves are mollusks whose visceral masses are enclosed in two hinged shells. Like gastropods, bivalves have a foot. Burrowing species of bivalves are equipped with siphons, extensions of the mantle that help pull water over the gills. Most bivalves are filter feeders whose gills are equipped with mucus to grab bits of food in the water.

In cephalopods, the foot is located near the animal's head. Examples of cephalopods include squid, octopuses, and nautiluses. Most octopuses are solitary animals that crawl on the seafloor looking for food. On the Gorda Escarpment, a plateau off the coast of California, thousands of octopuses lay their eggs and guard over them. Squid are more mobile than octopuses, swimming aggressively in the water in search of food. The vampire squid is a newly discovered deepwater animal that shows characteristics of both squid and octopuses.

In the marine environment, crustaceans, animals with exoskeletons and bodies divided into segments, make up the largest group of arthropods. Isopods, amphipods, copepods, shrimp, crabs, and lobsters are some typical crustaceans. Small crustaceans, such as isopods, amphipods, and copepods, are the dominant animals in phytoplankton. Shrimp, crabs, and lobsters live on the seafloor in deep-water areas. Around geothermal vents, shrimp are blind, an adaptation to the dark environment, but possess pigmented tissue that enables them to sense the locations of geothermal vents.

Echinoderms are abundant on the deep seafloor. Sea stars live above and within the silty sediments alongside sea cucumbers, long echinoderms that resemble fat worms. Sea stars and brittle stars are flattened animals with mouths on the ventral surface and anuses on the dorsal side. Sea cucumbers are elongated, so their mouths are located on the anterior end. Crinoids are ancient echinoderms that look like stalked flowers.

5

Fish
Vertebrates in Every Region of the Open Ocean

*V*ertebrates, animals with backbones, include *fish,
amphibians, reptiles, birds,* and *mammals.* Fish, the
largest group, are inhabitants of all marine environments
where they play critically important roles in food webs as
predators and prey. The locations of different kinds of fish are
determined by the physical and chemical characteristics of
bodies of water.

One of the delineating characteristics of fish habitats is
water depth. Oceans can be divided into layers, or zones, that
extend from the surface of the water down to extreme depths
where no light can penetrate. The epipelagic or upper zone is
home to many familiar species, including most food fish. The
mesopelagic zone, the midwater region, contains unusual
creatures such as fish with enlarged eyes and glowing spots.
In the bathypelagic zone, fish have special adaptations that
allow them to survive tough conditions. Here the water pressure is immense, the temperature cold, the oxygen supply
low, the food scarce, and the natural light absent. Many of the
creatures in this area have bioluminescent structures called
photophores positioned over their bodies in strategic locations. These "glow in the dark" fish are very common in the
deep ocean, and they use this adaptation to attract and capture prey, to frighten or confuse potential predators, and for
communication.

Epipelagic Fish

Flying fish, members of the family Exocoetidae, are some of
the most visible residents of the epipelagic zone. Capable of
incredible leaps, flying fish soar in the air as far as the length
of a football field. Because they are attracted to the lights of
boats, the night-flying species of this family have been known

to sail out of the ocean and literally into the laps of passengers. All members of this family have elongated, winglike pectoral fins that enable them to glide in the air. One of the largest species of flying fish, the one-foot-long (30.5 cm) *Cypselurus heterurus,* has a dark blue back, silver sides and belly, and a gray dorsal fin, an example of *countershading.* Like other flying fish, *Cypselurus heterurus* feeds on small plants and animals.

Fish of the family Scombridae, tunas and mackerel, also live in the first 656 feet (200 m) of water. Members of this family are muscular and speedy endurance swimmers whose bodies are covered by velvety skin and tiny scales. Tuna can weigh several hundred pounds, like the one shown in the lower color insert on page C-5. The yellow tuna (*Thunnus albacares*), found worldwide in tropical seas, is one of the fastest fish. Clocked at speeds of 40 miles per hour (64 km per hr), the yellow tuna can travel as far as 150 miles in a single day.

Fig. 5.1   Yellow or yellowfin tuna (Thunnus albacares) *are fast-swimming fish that can reach speeds of 40 miles per hour.* (Courtesy of William High, NMFS, NOAA)

Bony Fish Anatomy

All bony fish share many physical characteristics, which are labeled in Figure 5.2. One of their distinguishing features is scaly skin. Scales on fish overlap one another, much like shingles on a roof, protecting the skin from damage and slowing the movement of water into or out of the fish's body.

Bony fish are outfitted with fins that facilitate maneuvering and positioning in the water. The fins, which are made of thin membranes supported by stiff pieces of cartilage, can be folded down or held upright. Fins are named for their location: Dorsal fins are on the back, a caudal fin is at the tail, and an anal fin is on the ventral side. Two sets of lateral fins are located on the sides of the fish, the pectoral fins are toward the head, and the pelvic fins are near the tail. The caudal fin moves the fish forward in the water, and the others help change direction and maintain balance.

Although fish dine on a wide assortment of food, most species are predators whose mouths contain small teeth for grasping prey. Nutrients from digested food are distributed through the body by a system of closed blood vessels. The circulation of blood is powered by a muscular two-chambered heart. Blood entering the heart is depleted of oxygen and filled with carbon dioxide, a waste product of metabolism. Blood collects in the upper chamber, the atrium, before it is pushed into the ventricle. From the ventricle, it travels to the gills where it picks up oxygen and gets rid of its carbon dioxide. Water exits through a single gill slit on the side of the head. The gill slits of fish are covered with a protective flap, the operculum.

In many bony fish, some gases in the blood are channeled into another organ, the swim bladder. This organ is essentially a gas bag that helps the fish control its depth by adjusting its buoyancy. A fish can float higher in the water by increasing the volume of gas in the swim bladder. To sink, the fish reduces the amount of gas in the bladder.

Most bony fish reproduce externally. Females lay hundreds of eggs in the water, then males swim by and release milt, a fluid containing sperm, on the eggs. Fertilization occurs in the open water, and the parents swim away, leaving the eggs unprotected. Not all of the eggs are fertilized, and many that are fertilized will become victims of predators, so only a small percentage of eggs hatch.

Fig. 5.2 The special features of bony fish include bony scales (a), opercula (b), highly maneuverable fins (c), a tail with its upper and lower lobes usually of equal size (d), a swim bladder that adjusts the fish's buoyancy (e), nostrils (f), pectoral fins (g), a pelvic fin (h), an anal fin (i), lateral lines (j), dorsal fins (k), and a stomach (l).

Features of Bony Fish

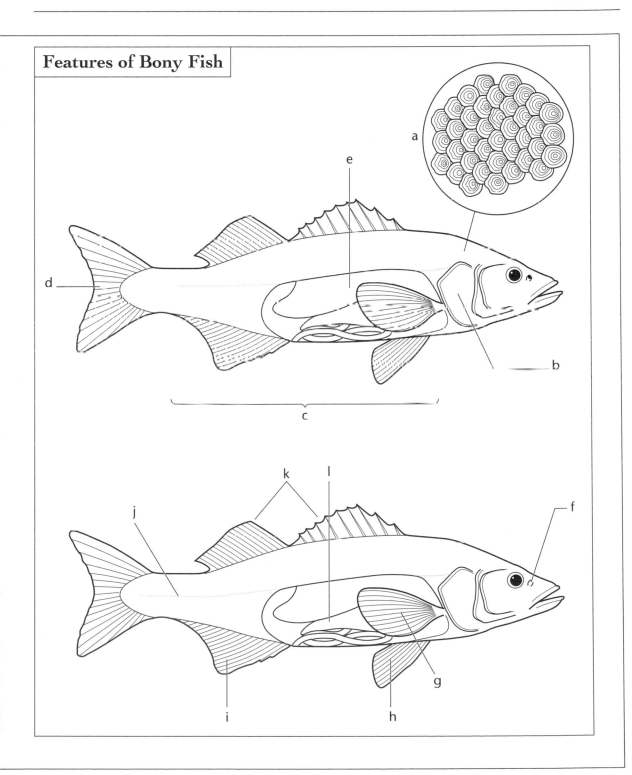

Growing to 6.6 feet (2 m) in length, this fish has a dark metallic back and caudal fin with a yellow-and-silver belly and sides that can be seen in the photo. At night yellow tuna are active at the surface of the water where they feed on other fish, crustaceans, and squid.

The wahoo (*Acanthocybium solandri*) is another member of the Scombridae family. This warm-water, torpedo-shaped fish preys on flying fish. Extremely sharp, serrated teeth, elongated jaws, and a beaklike snout make the wahoo a formidable predator that may hunt alone or in loose aggregates.

Another family of fish, the Coryphaenidae, also feed on flying fish. The common dolphinfish (*Coryphaena hippurus*) lives worldwide in tropical and temperate waters, from the surface of the ocean down to about 295 feet (90 m) deep. These colorful fish, which grow to around 6.6 feet (2 m) in length, are black dorsally, various shades of blues and greens laterally, and white and yellow on the ventral surface. The dolphinfish has a slender, flattened shape, with a blunt head and a jaw that protrudes forward. A large dorsal fin runs from the head down the entire length of the fish.

Living in tropical and subtropical waters, the long-snouted sailfish patrols waters about 98.4 feet (30 m) below the ocean surface. The bones around the nose of a sailfish form a spearlike bill that these fast-swimming fish use to stun their prey. The common name "sailfish" comes from the unusually tall first dorsal fin. The Indo-Pacific sailfish (*Istiophorus platypterus*) is found in tropical and temperate waters of the Pacific and Indian Oceans. Growing to a maximum size of 4.3 feet (1.3 m) and 220.5 pounds (100 kg), *Istiophorus* feeds on crustaceans, cephalopods, and smaller fish.

A part-time resident of the epipelagic zone, the swordfish of the family Xiphiidae resembles a sailfish. The nose of this large predator of tropical and subtropical waters forms a pointed, sharp-edged sword. The scaleless body of an adult swordfish can reach lengths of 14.8 feet (4.5 m). A swordfish has a sleek, tunalike body shape and a deeply forked tail, a combination of traits that makes it a powerful swimmer. This strength and speed, along with the fish's built-in sword, give rise to a formidable hunter. With very few predators of its own, the swordfish hunts and eats bluefish, mackerel, and squid. Swordfish (*Xiphias gladius*) can be found in subtropical oceans at depths that range from the water surface down to 2,624.7 feet (800 m).

A fish that lives in warm waters between the ocean's surface and depths of 984.3 feet (300 m) is the ocean sunfish (*Mola mola*), shown in the upper color insert on page C-6. Like other members of the family Molidae, the scaleless body of an ocean sunfish is covered with very thick, elastic skin. The mouth of the fish is small, filled with teeth that are fused into a parrotlike beak for feeding on mollusks, crustaceans, brittle stars, and small fish. Much of a sunfish's day is spent near the surface, lying on its side or swimming upright with its dorsal fin protruding from the water. Ocean sunfish, which are found around the world, can attain lengths of 9.8 to 13.1 feet (3 to 4 m). Adults have few predators, but the juveniles are preyed on by sea lions.

The epipelagic zone is also home to several cartilaginous fish. The tiger shark and oceanic whitetip shark, both of the family Carcharhinidae, spend the majority of their time in the open ocean, ranging from the surface down to the margin of the mesopelagic zone. The oceanic whitetip shark (*Carcharhinus longimanus*) has a large, rounded dorsal fin and paddlelike pectoral fins that are tipped in white. This shark, which grows up to 13 feet (4 m) long and weighs 350 pounds (159 kg), is found worldwide in tropical and subtropical waters. The whitetip shark is known to be very aggressive and has been implicated in open-ocean attracks on humans after air or sea disasters. The favorite preys of whitetip sharks are fish, stingrays, sea turtles, seabirds, squid, and crustaceans. They also feed on the carcasses of dead mammals.

Sharks from the family Lamnidae (the mackerel or white sharks) are epipelagic animals that sometimes swim in the upper portion of the mesopelagic zone. Although they are gray dorsally, the fish get their common name from their white bellies. The porbeagle (*Lamna nasus*), reaching lengths of 11.5 feet (3.5 m), can be found in temperate water from the ocean surface down to depths of 1,345.8 feet (715 m). The porbeagle is a stout shark with a white belly, large, dark eyes, and a sharp, cone-shaped snout. Swimming alone or in schools, porbeagles feed on smaller fish, other sharks, and squid.

Another Lamnidae shark, the short-fin mako (*Isurus oxyrinchus*), is an open-ocean inhabitant that is commonly seen near the surface of the water. The cobalt-blue mako grows to lengths of six to eight feet (2.4 m) and weighs about 300 pounds (136.1 kg), although one of the largest makos captured weighed in at 1,000 pounds (453.6 kg). Known as fast and agile swimmers, these sharks hunt mackerel, tuna, and sardines.

The basking shark (*Cetorhinus maximus*), family Cetorhinidae, is the second-largest fish in the world. Reaching lengths of 33 feet (10 m), basking sharks swim in the upper layers of the ocean with their huge mouths held open. To swim, these mottled-gray giants move their entire bodies back and forth, not just their tails like some sharks. Despite their fierce appearance, basking sharks are nonaggressive filter feeders. As a shark swims, water flows into the mouth, over racks of gills that almost completely surround the throat and out through openings called the gill slits. Tiny hooks on the gills catch planktonic organisms such as copepods, fish eggs, and larvae of shellfish.

The pelagic stingray (*Dasyatis violacea*), family Dasyatididae, is another cartilaginous, epipelagic fish. Most rays and skates spend their days on the bottom of the ocean, buried in mud and sand, but the pelagic stingray prefers to swim near the surface of open water. This purple-colored stingray has a diamond-shaped body with a rounded snout. A native of subtropical waters, the pelagic stingray has a venomous spine on its tail, like other stingrays. It feeds on squid, crustaceans, fish, and cnidarians, often from an upside-down position.

Mesopelagic Fish

The first fish likely to be spotted in the midwater environment of the open ocean is the lantern fish, a member of the family Myctophidae. Lantern fish stand out because their bodies are covered with photophores that generate light. The amount and pattern of light differs in each species of the family. To find

◀ *Minerals spewing from a hydrothermal vent from a tall chimney around the vent opening.* (Courtesy of OAR/National Undersea Research Program, P. Rona, NOAA)

▲ *Inactive hydrothermal vents cover an area of deep seafloor near Hawaii.* (Courtesy of OAR/National Undersea Research Program, G. McMurtry, NOAA)

▲ *Golden coral grows on the rocky seafloor off Hawaii in water that is more than 1,000 feet (304.8 m) deep.* (Courtesy of OAR/National Undersea Research Program, NOAA)

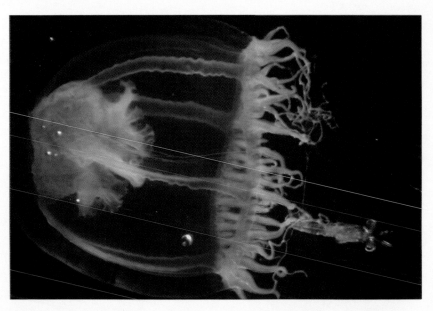

▲ *Jellyfish are carnivores that prey on small fish and invertebrates.*
(Matt Wilson/Jay Clark, NOAA, NMFS, AFSC)

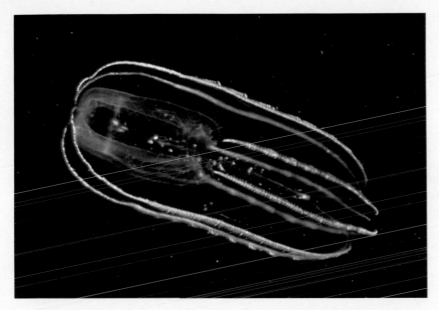

▲ *Many ctenophores, or comb jellies, are bioluminescent.* (Courtesy of OAR/National Undersea Research Program, NOAA)

▲ *These clams live in beds around a hydrothermal vent 9,186.4 feet (2,900 m) below the water's surface.* (Courtesy of OAR/National Undersea Research Program, A. Malahoff, NOAA)

▲ *Krill, tiny crustaceans, are vital links in the Southern Ocean food webs.* (Courtesy of Jamie Hall, Sanctuary Collection, NOAA)

▲ *A spider crab lives among mussels and tubeworms near a geothermal vent.* (Courtesy of OAR/National Undersea Research Program, I. MacDonald, NOAA)

▲ *Crinoids live on a dead sponge in water off Hawaii that is more than 5,000 feet (1,524 m) deep.* (Courtesy of OAR/National Undersea Research Program, J. Moore, NOAA)

▲ *A diver frees a 600-pound (270 kg) tuna that is ensnared in a fish trap.* (Courtesy of United Nations Food and Agriculture Organization, Danilo Cedrone, NOAA)

▲ *An ocean sunfish* (Mola mola) *swims in the epipelagic zone.*
(Courtesy of NOAA, Sanctuary Collection)

▲ *A duck-billed eel swims over the floor on an Indo-Pacific Ocean
continental slope.* (Courtesy of OAR/National Undersea Research
Program, J. Moore, NOAA)

▲ Fish that live in the deep sea are often white or transparent.
(Courtesy of Matt Wilson/Jay Clark, NOAA, NMFS, AFSC)

▲ A blue-footed booby eyes a nesting pair of waved albatrosses.
(Courtesy of Rosalind Cohen, NODC, NOAA)

▲ *Markings on the tails of individual humpback whales are distinctive.* (Courtesy of OAR/National Undersea Research Program, R. Wicklund, NOAA)

▲ *A killer whale "spy-hops" through an opening in the ice.* (Courtesy of NOAA's Ark Collection)

a potential mate, a lantern fish searches for another fish that has a light pattern to match its own. Many lantern fish migrate to the surface at night to feed on copepods, shrimp, and amphipods. The northern lampfish (*Stenobrachius leucopsarus*) is a five-inch-long (12 cm) species that lives in the California Current System from Baja, California, to Japan.

The viperfish, family Chauliodontidae, is another light-producing midwater resident. The long, sharp teeth of a viperfish are responsible for the animal's common name. Four fanglike teeth on the upper jaw and pointed, widely spaced teeth on the lower jaw enable viperfish to capture many kinds of prey. The body is flattened and covered with large, thin scales and luminescent spots. The Pacific viperfish (*Chauliodus macouni*) has a hinged jaw that allows it to swallow extremely large prey. Growing to a maximum length of 12 inches (30 cm), the Pacific viperfish sits with its large mouth wide open like a trap, waiting on its next meal to swim in. This strategy works well for the predator since other fish cannot see it lurking in the dark water.

Fish of the family Stomiidae, the dragonfish, also wait for prey with fanglike teeth. Dragonfish are fierce predators, even though adults are very small. The deep-sea dragonfish (*Grammatostomias flagellibarba*), found in tropical waters around the world, is only about six inches (15.2 cm) long, but the short body is equipped with a large head filled with sharp teeth. Attached to this little fish's chin is a long barbel that has a glowing tip. The dragonfish flashes the tip on and off as a luminous lure to attract prey. Once a curious fish wanders close enough to investigate the lure, the dragonfish grabs it. Members of the dragonfish family spend much of the daytime hours in water as deep as 5,000 feet (1,500 m), but at night they travel to the midwater region to hunt for food.

Another large-mouth occupant of the midwater region is the hatchetfish of the family Sternoptychidae. This thin, flat-sided fish, whose body is shaped like the blade of a hatchet, has a mouth filled with tiny, sharp teeth. Spiny projections stick out of the sides of the hatchetfish's body. The hatchetfish uses light-producing photophores to both attract prey and signal mates. Each species of hatchetfish has its own particular pattern of light. The deep-sea hatchetfish (*Argyropelecus gigas*), a four-inch-long (10 cm) species, has upward-pointing eyes to help it search for food, especially plankton and copepods, that may fall downward from the surface of the ocean. Deep-sea hatchetfish live in tropical and temperate waters worldwide.

An unusual creature that inhabits the midwater region is the snipe eel, family Nemichthyidae. These three- to four-foot-long (0.91 to 1.2 m) fish have slender bodies that may be 75 times longer than they are thick, ending with a tail that tapers to a thread. The top and lower jaws of snipe eels have unusual curvatures, giving them the appearance of duck bills. To catch food, this fish swims with its mouth open, snagging the antennae of shrimp with its sharp teeth. The slender snipe eel (*Nemichthys scolopaceus*), generally found in tropical and temperate seas, can grow as long as five feet (1.5 m), yet weigh

Shark Anatomy

Although there are many kinds of sharks, they all are similar anatomically. A shark's digestive system begins at the mouth, which is filled with teeth. Shark teeth are continuously produced, and at any time a shark may have 3,000 teeth arranged in six to 20 rows. As older teeth are lost from the front rows, younger ones move forward and replace them. Teeth are adapted to specific kinds of food. Depending on their species, sharks may have thin, daggerlike teeth for holding prey; serrated, wedge-shaped teeth for cutting and tearing; or small, conical teeth that can crush animals in shells.

The internal skeletons of sharks are made of cartilage, a lightweight and flexible bonelike material. Their external surfaces are very tough and rugged. Sharks have extremely flexible skin that is covered with placoid scales, each of which is pointed and has a rough edge on it. Shark fins are rigid and cannot be folded down like the fins of bony fish.

Like other aquatic organisms, sharks get the oxygen they need to live from the water. Compared to air, water contains a small percentage of dissolved oxygen. Surface waters may contain five milliliters of oxygen per liter of water, dramatically less than the 210 ml of oxygen per liter of air that is available to land animals. To survive, fish must be very efficient at removing and concentrating the oxygen in water.

In aquatic organisms, gills carry out the function of lungs in terrestrial animals. To respire, sharks pull water in through their mouths and *spiracles,* holes on top of their

only a few ounces. A similar fish, the duck-billed eel shown in the lower color insert on page C-6, is a resident of continental slopes of the Indo-Pacific seas. This long, flattened fish is gray with black edges and a gray-black snout.

The oarfish, family Regalecidae, the longest bony fish in the ocean, also occupies the midwater region. The oarfish can grow to 50 feet (15.2 m) in length and can weigh as much as 100 pounds (45.4 kg). Its pelvic fin is one extremely long ray. To catch tiny crustaceans in the water, oarfish take water into their small, toothless mouths, then strain it over gill rakers, tiny projections that prevent prey from escaping through the gills. Fish that are carnivores typically have short, widely spaced gill rakers. In fish that eat plankton, the structures are long, thin, and much more numerous.

heads. The water passes over their gills and exits through the gill slits on the sides of the head. Most species of sharks can pump water over their gills by opening and closing their mouths. Some sharks, the "ram ventilators," must swim continuously to move water over their gills. Oxygen in water is picked up by tiny blood vessels in the gills, then carried to the heart, a small two-chambered, S-shaped tube. From there, oxygenated blood is pumped to the rest of the body.

Sharks fertilize their eggs internally. Males transfer sperm to females using modified pelvic fins. Some species are *oviparous*, which means the female lays fertilized eggs. Shark eggs may be deposited in lagoons or shallow reef water, where they incubate for six to 15 months. Many of the eggs' cases are equipped with hairy or leathery tendrils that help hold them to rocks or plants. Other species are *viviparous*, so the embryos develop inside the mother and are born alive. Several species are *ovoviviparous*, which means that the embryo develops inside an egg within the female's body. The egg hatches inside the mother, the hatchling eats the yolk and any unfertilized eggs, then is born alive.

Shark populations are relatively small compared to other kinds of fish. One reason is because shark reproduction rates are low. Unlike fish and many of the invertebrates, a female shark produces only a few offspring each year. In addition, the gestation period, time when the embryo develops inside the mother, of viviparous species is long.

One member of the oarfish family the king of the herrings (*Regalecus glesne*), lives in depths of up to 3,280.8 feet (1,000 m). The head and body of this fish are silver with blue streaks, and the dorsal fin is crimson in color. Favorite foods of the king of the herrings include small fish, crustaceans, and squid.

Sharks can also be found in the mesopelagic zone. Cat sharks, family Scyliorhinidae, have flat heads and long, cat-like eyes that glow when light hits them. Because their eyes are extremely sensitive to light, cat sharks are successful predators in nearly dark conditions. The file-tail cat shark (*Parmaturus xaniurus*) is a relatively small shark that ranges between 12 to 40 inches (30 to 100 cm) in length. This shark gets its name from the file-like projections that stick out of its body. The file-tail cat shark prowls the ocean bottom searching for crustaceans and fish to eat.

Another type of shark, the mackerel or white shark of the family Lamnidae, inhabits the midwater regions. Members of this family have crescent-shaped tails with the lower lobe slightly shorter than the upper one. The most widely recognized species in family Lamnidae is the great white shark (*Carcharodon carcharias*). The dorsal surface of the great white shark is dark while the belly is white, and adult sharks grow to lengths of 21.3 feet (6.5 m) and have large, serrated teeth that are triangular in shape. These sharks are very aggressive feeders and will eat other sharks, fish, seals, and sea turtles. Even though great white sharks swim as deep as 4,200 feet (1,280 m), they occasionally come to the surface, and they are notable as the only species that ever raises their heads out of water, possibly to get a better view of their prey.

Ranging from the continental slope to depths of 6,561.7 feet (2,000 m), another species of shark found in the mid-ocean region is the six-gilled shark (*Hexanchus griseus*) of the family Hexanchidae. Most sharks have five gill slits rather than the six found in all members of this family, thus the origin of the common name. Growing to a length of 18 feet (5.5 m), this is one of the largest carnivorous sharks. Six-gilled sharks, found all over the world, are very slow swimmers, but they have the unusual ability to change colors to blend in with their surroundings. During the day these sharks stay in deep water but move to shallower regions at night to feed on cephalopods, fish, crustaceans, and marine mammals.

A relative of the sharks, the ratfish of the family Chimaeridae, is also associated with the continental slope and deep waters. The ratfish, known to some as the shortnose chimaera, feeds on mollusks, crustaceans, worms, echinoderms, and small fish. One representative of this family, the spotted ratfish (*Hydrolagus colliei*), has smooth skin, large green eyes, a spotted brown body, and a pointed tail. Females, which are larger than males, can grow up to 3.3 feet (1 m) in length. Spotted ratfish prefer cold waters near the bottom of the ocean. A dorsal spine and a strong, chisel-like plate of teeth in the fish's jaws can cause painful wounds.

Bathypelagic Fish

Many families of fish live in more than one zone of the ocean, making vertical trips from one region to the other. Members of the family Sebastidae, the rockfish and thornyheads, travel among the epipelagic, mesopelagic, and bathypelagic regions during their lives. Rockfish can also be found around the coral reefs and kelp beds feeding on plankton, krill, shrimp, crabs, squid, and other fish. The shortspine thornyhead (*Sebastolobus alascanus*) is a long-lived species and has been known to reach 115 years of age. This elongated, bright red fish generally does not exceed 31.2 inches (80 cm) in length. Most of the time, this species swims just above the soft, muddy bottom of the ocean floor.

Many of the fish of the bathypelagic zone are found on the continental slope. Skates, members of the family Rajidae, live on the floor of the deep sea. All skates and rays are cartilaginous fish rather than bony fish. Their flat bodies and winglike pectoral fins make them easily recognizable. The majority of the skates and rays are described as demersal since they stay near the bottom of the ocean floor, some even buried in the mud. Bottom-dwelling skates and rays cannot breathe by drawing water into their mouths, which are located on the ventral surface and usually flattened in shape. To compensate, these animals have openings called *spiracles* that are located just behind their eyes. Water drawn in through the spiracles flows over the gills, keeping the blood oxygenated. The deepwater ray (*Rajella bathyphilia*) is usually shorter than 3.3 feet (1 m) in length. Another member of the Rajidae family, the white skate (*Bathyraja spinosissima*), lives on the continental slope.

The blob sculpin (*Psychrolutes phrictus*), or fathead, of the family Psychrolutidae is a demersal fish. The blob sculpin, which grows to 27.6 inches (70 cm), has a thick, 27.6 inch (70 cm) long body that is covered with flabby, loose skin. Most of the time the blob sculpin waits on the ocean floor for crabs and mollusks to venture close enough to be captured.

The cold waters of continental slopes, ocean ridges, and seamounts are often associated with the Trachichthyidae family of fish, the slime heads. A particularly common and colorful representative, the orange roughy (*Hoplostethus atlanticus*) is one of the longest-lived fish in the oceans; one individual has been documented to be 149 years old. The orange roughy, which can grow to 29.5 inches (75 cm) in length, is a bright orange fish that frequents the waters above rough, steep substrates where it feeds on fish and crustaceans.

Fish that are permanent residents of the deep sea look very different from those of upper waters. Most are small, like the ones in the upper color insert on page C-7. Many deepwater fish lack color, a useless characteristic in a completely dark environment, and are white or transparent.

Gulper eels, family Eurypharyngidae, patrol the deep waters of the ocean. The pelican gulper eel (*Eurypharynx pelecanoides*) is found worldwide in temperate or tropical waters. Sometimes called the "umbrella-mouth gulper," this fish can unhinge its jaws wide enough to snare large prey. The pelican part of the name comes from the pouchlike lower jaw that expands to hold a catch, much like a pelican's pouch. The rest of the animal's body is snakelike and flaccid, growing to six feet (1.8 m) long, with tiny eyes and a small red light on the top of its tail. To catch food, this fish swims in circles so that the light on its tail will attract prey. Once prey gets close, the eel wraps the victim in its long tail and then consumes the animal. Like some other deepwater fish, the pelican eel keeps

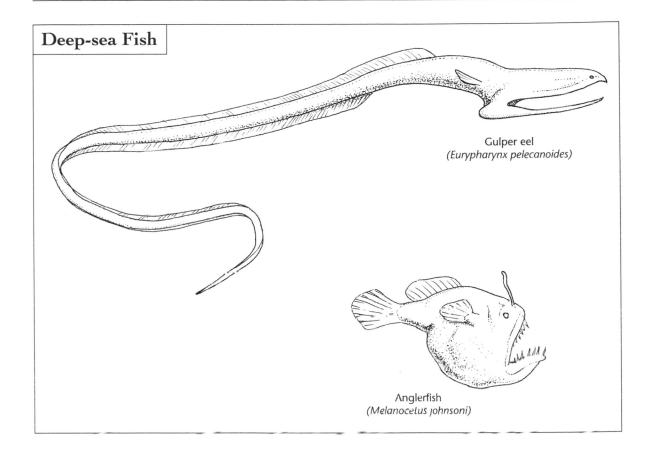

Deep-sea Fish

Gulper eel
(*Eurypharynx pelecanoides*)

Anglerfish
(*Melanocetus johnsoni*)

its big mouth agape most of the time and will eat almost anything that drifts in.

Sea anglers, family Ceratidae, may be some of the most bizarre-looking deep-sea fish. Most anglerfish, shown in Figure 5.3 with another type of deep-sea fish, are small, rounded animals that resemble tennis balls with fins. The first dorsal fin of an angler is elongated into what looks like a fishing lure on the end of a long string. The tip of the lure can be illuminated with photophores. As the angler flashes its lure on and off, it uses muscle contractions to wave the fin back and forth, very much like the actions of an angler with a fishing pole. When prey comes close to the lure, the fish snaps it up in its powerful jaws. Anglerfish have distensible stomachs, enabling them to swallow prey twice their own size. The giant female deep-sea angler (*Ceratias holboelli*), the largest member

Fig. 5.3 *Two examples of deep-sea fish are the gulper eel* (Eurypharynx pelecanoides) *and the anglerfish* (Melanocetus johnsoni).

of this family, grows to almost 40 inches (101.6 cm) in length. Her male counterpart, only about four inches (10.2 cm) long, uses his sharp teeth to attach to the female. Once joined, the male's blood vessels fuse with those of the female, and the two stay connected for the rest of their lives. Males who are unable to find a mate die of starvation.

Fish of the Abyss

The area of the ocean below 13,123.4 feet (4,000 m) is called the abyss, or the bottomless sea. Fish at these extreme depths have special adaptations to withstand high pressures, lack of food, complete darkness, and icy temperatures. One family, the Macrouridae, is commonly known as the rattails or grenadiers. Related to the cod family, these fish are so named because they have huge heads with large eyes and long, tapered tails that resemble those of rodents. Large rattails grow up to 3.3 feet (1 m) long, but the average size is around 31 inches (80 cm). The pointed snout of a rattail ends in a small barbel. Rattails are one of the few fish that have been seen in the vicinity of hydrothermal vents. In the northern Pacific, the gray-brown giant grenadier (*Albatrossia pectoralis*) can grow as long as 4.9 feet (1.5 m) and has been known to live to age 56.

Fish of the family Zoarcidae, the zoarcid fish, are a dominant group around hydrothermal vents. These slow-moving fish, which can grow to 3.3 feet (1 m) in length, are predatory and will eat everything from tube worms to shrimp. Two zoarcid genera, *Pachycara* and *Thermarces*, have been recovered from areas around active hydrothermal vents. *Thermarces cerberus*, commonly referred to as the ventfish, is white or pink in color and lacks scales over its body.

Zoarcid fish can tolerate a wide range of temperatures, even those below freezing. Presently scientists are researching the so-called antifreeze proteins found in the bodies of zoarcids to find out how these molecules absorb ice and lower the freezing point of blood. The production of sharp-edged ice particles in the tissues is one of the biggest dangers of cold temperatures. The discovery of such a protein might help doctors treat victims of frostbite or enable people to safely explore extremely cold regions.

Fangtooth, members of the family Anoplogastridae, are also called ogrefish. Armed with long, sharp teeth in an over-size mouth, these animals have a ferocious appearance. The fangtooth will eat almost anything, because food at this extreme depth is scarce, but fish, squid, and crustaceans are its favorite foods. The common fangtooth (*Anoplogaster cornuta*), which are about 5.8 inches (15 cm) in size, live world-wide in the waters of temperate and tropical zones.

Eelpouts are drab-colored, eel-like zoarcids that are normally bottom-dwellers. They have larger heads than true eels and thick, fleshy lips that make their facial expression look like they are pouting. Worldwide, these fish live among rocky crevices near the ocean bottom. The largest species are slightly less than 3.3 feet (1 m) long. The midwater eelpout (*Melanostigma pammelas*) has a weak skeleton and very little muscle. This fish frequently curls its long, thin body into a circle, perhaps a strategy to look un-fishlike and therefore avoid detection by predators. The midwater eelpout feeds on amphipods and shrimp.

The fish family Brotulidae includes *Abyssobrotula galatheae*, a species that was found in a Puerto Rican trench that is 27,467.2 feet (8,372 m) deep. Consequently *Abyssobrotula galatheae* lives in deeper water than any other known fish. This particular species resides in very deep regions of tropical and subtropical areas of all oceans. A peculiar-looking fish, *Abyssobrotula galatheae* has a short head that points down-ward, an enlarged snout, tiny eyes, and a tapering tail.

Conclusion

Fish are large, highly visible vertebrates in the open ocean. The populations of fish found within any region of the open ocean depend on factors such as climate, light, temperature, and pressure. To classify open-ocean fish, scientists often separate them into groups based on the depth of the water they inhabit.

Epipelagic zones of the ocean provide homes for thousands of species of fish, including flying fish, tuna, mackerel, dolphinfish, sailfish, swordfish, ocean sunfish, whitetip sharks, mako sharks, pelagic stingrays, and great white sharks. Most of these animals are adapted for fast-swimming lifestyles. Flying fish distinguish themselves with their ability to leap from the water and glide in the air on elongated pectoral fins. Sailfish and swordfish are large, powerful animals with spearlike adaptations for preying on fish. The slower-moving ocean sunfish spends much of its time floating in the surface waters.

Sharks of the epipelagic zone tend to be large, aggressive predators. The great white shark travels between the epipelagic and mesopelagic zones. Closely related to sharks are the stingrays and skates, most of which live in benthic environments. The pelagic stingray is an exception, swimming in the upper layers of the open ocean.

In the mesopelagic zone, many fish species show adaptations for low light and little food. The production of bioluminescent light within structures called photophores enhances the ability of fish to communicate in this dark zone. Species such as the northern lampfish use bioluminescent light to signal potential mates. Mesopelagic fish are armed with much longer, sharper fins than many shallow-water species. The viperfish has a mouth full of fangs that ensures potential prey will not escape.

Bathypelagic fish may display some of the most bizarre body shapes and adaptations known to science. Many species have extremely large mouths, sharp teeth, and small bodies, adaptations that give them the best possible chance of catching a meal with the least possible expenditure of energy. Bathypelagic fish tend to be slow-moving animals that sit and wait for prey instead of chasing it. Gulper eels, elongated fish with extremely large mouths, swim in circles to attract prey with lighted lures on the tips of their tails. Anglerfish use a similar approach but dangle their lures in front of their mouths.

At extreme water depth, the diversity of fish decreases dramatically. In the abyssal zone, very few species are found. Rattails are long, thin fish with lurelike barbels on their snouts. The northern giant grenadier is a rattail fish that is found around hydrothermal vents in the Pacific Ocean. Zoarcid fish are slow-moving, pale-skinned predators that can live in the hot water of deep-sea vents or the near-freezing waters of the abyss.

6

Reptiles, Birds, and Mammals
Rulers of the Oceanic Realm

eptiles, birds, and mammals are three groups of air-breathing vertebrates found in the open and deep oceans. Vertebrates are highly mobile animals, and many spend only part of their lives in the oceanic realm. Some are migratory, dividing their time between northern and southern latitudes. A good number travel to shallow water for seasonal activities, such as mating and molting. Depending on the species, marine vertebrates may return to land to raise their young or give birth to live offspring in the water.

What distinguishes oceanic vertebrates from others is that they spend the majority of their lives in deep, open water, far from land. As descendants of terrestrial ancestors, these organisms have developed special physical and behavioral adaptations for oceanic life. All of these air breathers are excellent swimmers, and some are proficient divers who can

Fig. 6.1   A food chain in the epipelagic zone begins with phytoplankton (a), the producers. Phytoplankton are consumed by zooplankton (b), which serve as food for small fish (c). Larger fish (d) eat the small fish; the larger fish are eaten by squid (e), one of the favorite foods of dolphins (f). Baleen whales (g) eat phytoplankton and zooplankton.

Food Chain

remain submerged for hours. As figure 6.1 indicates, vertebrates are usually the top predators in open-ocean food webs.

Bodies of oceanic vertebrates are protected from constant cold and wet conditions by several strategies. Thick layers of hair or feathers, waterproofed with oil, offer protection to many kinds of animals. In some cases, fat acts as insulation that helps prevent heat loss. High rates of metabolism, the chemical reactions in an organism's body, generate body heat.

Marine Reptiles

In the deep, open expanses of the ocean, two kinds of reptiles are right at home: sea snakes and marine turtles. Only one species of snake, the yellow-bellied sea snake (*Pelamis platurus*), is truly oceanic; most other species live over the continental shelf or near the coast. Yellow-bellied sea snakes inhabit the Pacific and Indian Oceans. Adapted for a life of swimming and floating, this snake has a flattened, paddlelike tail. On the dorsal surface, the snake is dark brown or gray, but the ventral side is bright yellow. Yellow-bellied sea snakes mate and give birth to live young in the water. Mature snakes reach lengths of three feet (90 cm). A gland in the snake's mouth excretes excess salt consumed during feeding.

A sea snake can lay on the water's surface by breathing through nostrils that are located high on the head and out of the water. Even though the sea snake is an air-breather, like all reptiles, it spends 90 percent of its time underwater. To keep water out of the respiratory tract when the snake is submerged, special valves cover the nostrils.

An excellent diver, *Pelamis platurus* is capable of staying underwater for periods of two to four hours, depending on its level of activity. While submerged, dissolved oxygen in the water travels through the snake's skin and enters the bloodstream. The scales of this snake fit together end to end, very much like brick pavers, with a little space between each scale. In terrestrial snakes, the scales overlap one another. The arrangement of a sea snake's scales leaves sections of skin exposed. The skin contains millions of tiny blood vessels and is capable of absorbing oxygen gas directly from the water.

Unwanted gases, including carbon dioxide and nitrogen, are released through the skin.

In the open-ocean food chain, the yellow-bellied sea snake is one of the top predators, consuming fish, birds, and invertebrates. The brightly colored snake has few predators of its own. In nature, bright coloration often signals danger, and in the case of the sea snake the signal is warranted. The skin of this snake apparently tastes bad because predators like large fish and seabirds often spit it out. In addition, the snake's venom is extremely toxic, much more so than the venom of terrestrial snakes. Sea snakes are slow swimmers, so they need potent venom that quickly immobilizes their prey and prevents its escape. Yellow-bellied sea-snake toxin, a nerve poison that interferes with the transmission of electrical signals from nerves to muscles, is injected into the victim through small, nonretractable fangs.

Since they cannot catch prey by chasing it, sea snakes float at the water's surface and wait for prey to come to them. Fish have a natural tendency to hide in the shade of anything floating on the water, so the very presence of the snake attracts prey within striking range. Floating snakes may form huge aggregates that cover miles of the Pacific Ocean.

Marine turtles are reptiles that have many of the characteristics of their terrestrial relatives, but they are generally larger. Worldwide, there are eight species of marine turtles. The three most common in the open ocean include the Atlantic leatherback (*Dermochelys coriacea*), the Atlantic hawksbill (*Eretmochelys imbricata*) and the green sea turtle (*Chelonia mydas*).

Despite its name, the green sea turtle is brown in color. The common name for this animal is derived from the green fat inside its body. Green sea turtles are 31.5 to 47.2 inches (80 to 120 cm) long and weigh 59 to 113.4 pounds (130 to 250 kg). Adults feed on sea grass and algae, but juveniles prefer shellfish and jellyfish. Green sea turtles make their homes in tropical and temperate regions of the Atlantic, Pacific, and Indian Oceans.

The life history of a green sea turtle is typical of many marine turtles. During breeding season, a female lays several clutches of eggs on the beach, depositing about one hundred

Marine Reptile Anatomy

Reptiles are not usually associated with marine environments. In fact, of the 6,000 known species of reptiles, only about 1 percent inhabits the sea. Members of this select group include lizards, crocodiles, turtles, and snakes. Each of these organisms shares many of the same anatomical structures that are found in all reptiles: They are cold-blooded, air-breathing, scaled animals that reproduce by internal fertilization. Yet, to live in salt water, this subgroup has evolved some special adaptations not seen in terrestrial reptiles.

In turtles, the shell is the most unique feature. The lightweight, streamline shape of the shell forms a protective enclosure for the vital organs. The ribs and backbone of the turtle are securely attached to the inside of the shell. The upper part of the shell, the carapace, is covered with horny plates that connect to the shell's bottom, the plastron. Extending out from the protective shell are the marine turtle's legs, which have been modified into paddle-like flippers capable of propelling it at speeds of up to 35 miles per hour (56 kph) through the water. These same legs are cumbersome on land, making the animals slow and their movements awkward.

Most air-breathing vertebrates cannot drink salty water because it causes dehydration and kidney damage. Seawater contains sodium chloride and other salts in concentrations three times greater than blood and body fluids. Many marine reptiles drink seawater, so their bodies rely on special salt-secreting glands to handle the excess salt. To reduce the load of salt in body fluids, these glands produce and excrete fluid that is twice as salty as seawater. The glands work very quickly, processing and getting rid of salt about 10 times faster than kidneys. Salt glands are located on the head, often near the eyes.

There are more than 50 species of sea snakes that thrive in marine environments. Sea snakes possess adaptations such as nasal valves and close-fitting scales around the mouth that keep water out during diving. Flattened tails that look like small paddles easily propel these reptiles through the water. The lungs in sea snakes are elongated, muscular air sacs that are able to store oxygen. In addition, sea snakes can take in oxygen through the skin. Their adaptations to the marine environment enable sea snakes to stay submerged from 30 minutes up to two hours; however, this ability comes at a cost. Because marine snakes routinely swim to the surface to breathe, they use more energy and have higher metabolic rates than land snakes. To balance their high energy consumption, they require more food than their terrestrial counterparts.

Finally, crocodiles usually occupy freshwater, but there are some species that live in brackish water (in between salt water and freshwater) and salt water. These animals have salivary glands that have been modified to excrete salt. Their tails are flattened for side-to-side swimming and their toes possess well-developed webs. Saltwater crocodiles are equipped with valves at the back of the throat that enable them to open their mouths and feed underwater without flooding their lungs.

eggs in each clutch. The eggs incubate in the sand for almost two months, then young hatchlings climb to the top of the nest and scramble to the water.

The trip from nest to water is hazardous, and many hatchlings are picked off by predators. Those that make it to the sea spend the next several years in the open ocean. Even in the deep waters, birds, fish, and marine mammals prey on the young turtles, reducing their numbers. After several years, surviving turtles move to nearshore habitats where they feed on grasses and algae, remaining in the shallow waters until they are old enough to breed, somewhere between 25 and 50 years of age.

During breeding season, males and females migrate to nesting beaches, locations that are often thousands of miles from feeding grounds. Courtship and mating occur in the sea near the beaches. At night, when temperatures are at their coolest, females climb onto shore and lay clutches of fertilized eggs. Before egg-laying begins, each female digs a nest in the sand with her powerful hind flippers. Once the nest is prepared, the turtle deposits one hundred or so billiard-ball-sized eggs. After carefully covering the nest with sand, the female returns to the nearby water, resting but not feeding. Two weeks later she returns to shore again, chooses another location, and lays another clutch of eggs. Each female may lay several clutches in one breeding season. When egg-laying is over, the female migrates back to her feeding grounds and resumes normal life. Of all the eggs she lays, only one percent lives to sexual maturity.

The Atlantic hawksbill is dark green-brown in color and measures 21.7 to 37.4 inches (55 to 95 cm) in length, weighing about 121.3 pounds (55 kg). A narrow, hawklike jaw accounts for this turtle's common name. Hawksbills dine on sponges, mollusks, and sea urchins. They can be found living in tropical and subtropical waters of the Atlantic, Pacific, and Indian Oceans.

Leatherback sea turtles are black to dark blue, 47 to 82.7 inches (120 to 210 cm) long, and weigh up to 1,984 pounds (900 kg). Instead of a hard shell like other turtles, the leatherback's shell is made of smooth, tough skin. These large animals dive deeply to search for squid and jellyfish in the warm regions of the Atlantic, Indian, and Pacific Oceans.

Seabirds

Since the seas cover 70 percent of the Earth's surface, it is not surprising that several types of birds make their homes there. Oceanic seabirds are so highly adapted to a marine lifestyle that they only travel to shore to lay eggs and raise young. Varying widely in size, oceanic seabirds include the largest bird, the albatross, whose wingspan reaches 12 feet (3.7 m), as well as the tiny petrel, whose wingspan is only a few inches. Penguins, boobies, gannets, auks, puffins, shearwaters, fulmars, prions (whale birds), razorbills, murres, dovekies, guillemots, auklets, gulls, terns, and some ducks and geese spend the majority of their lives above the open sea.

The distribution of seabirds varies, depending on climate, geography, weather, and oceanic water conditions. Seabirds are more numerous in the Southern Hemisphere than the Northern. This may simply be because a larger proportion of the Southern Hemisphere is oceanic or it could have to do with the strong, constant winds that are characteristic of southern waters. Seabirds depend on winds to help them glide, a method of flying that uses less energy than wing-flapping. In addition, there are more birds near the poles than in tropical zones, a distribution that may be due to less competition for food in the polar zones or the dense populations of zooplankton found near the pole.

Seabirds have perfected several highly effective feeding techniques. Storm petrels, terns, and jaegers fly low over the surface of the water grabbing prey with their feet. Fulmars sit on the water and wait for prey to get close to them. Penguins, auks, and shearwaters are pursuit divers that swim underwater, propelling themselves after prey with with their short, strong wings. Gannets, boobies, pelicans, and terns do not swim underwater; these birds plunge into the sea from high in the air, depending on the momentum of their dive to plunge them deep enough to snare prey.

Food is scarce in the open ocean, and many birds travel all the time to find enough food to survive. When food, such as a school of fish or the carcass of a dead animal, is located, the bird gorges. After such a feast, there may be long periods of famine before food can be located again. This feeding style of "feast or famine" is very different from the feeding habits of terrestrial birds that are able to eat on a regular basis.

The scarcity of food explains why seabirds are not picky eaters. Most species will consume anything they can find, including fish, crustaceans, mollusks, and eggs. Finicky or specialized eaters could not survive in an environment with so little food. The only time that seabirds are selective about the food they eat is when they are raising their young. Many seabird parents feed their offspring only one type of food, such as fish or squid.

In the Northern Hemisphere, some of the favorite feeding grounds for seabirds are off the coast of Newfoundland. These waters are filled with nutrients supplied through upwellings, so they support large populations of phytoplankton, copepods, and krill. Some of the species of seabirds that feed near Newfoundland only visit the area during their nonbreeding season. Other species breed there, using the shallow-water areas off the coast as their nursery.

Seabirds are not adversely affected by bad weather. The albatross even depends on storms to help it travel long distances. Without the strong winds produced by storms, albatrosses would have to expend too much energy flapping their wings to make it from one feeding ground to another.

Many seabirds migrate seasonally, some making incredibly long trips. The Arctic tern travels from the Arctic to the Antarctic yearly, a round trip of more than 20,000 miles (32,286.8 km). Each year, the sooty shearwater makes a circuit around the Pacific Ocean and then another one around the Atlantic Ocean. Wilson's Petrel, a small bird about the size of a starling, annually flies from breeding places in Antarctic to waters off Newfoundland and Nova Scotia.

Birds that are members of the family Sulidae are referred to as "boobies" in the tropics and "gannets" in northern waters. Found all over the world, Sulidae fly high above the water looking for food. When prey is spotted, they dive in with a splash, continuing the chase underwater. Sulidae are not damaged by high-impact dives because air sacks located under their skin cushion blows. Northern gannets (*Sula bassanus*) are about 40 inches (100 cm) long, with white feathers on their bodies and upper wings and black wingtips.

The tubenoses of the order Procellariiformes are a group of oceanic birds that include petrels, albatrosses, and shearwaters. Each member has nostrils that are fused into a single tube that runs along the top of its bill. This tube enables the bird to drink salt water and dispose of the excess salt. Salt accumulates inside the specialized tube, and then the bird sneezes it out. The distinctive tube structure also detects odors and helps the bird to determine the strength of air currents. Each tube-nosed bird has an oil-producing gland in its stomach that is used to feed newly hatched young. Because the oil has an unpleasant odor, adults also use it for defense, regurgitating the foul-smelling substance through the mouth and nostrils when threatened.

Albatrosses are the largest seabirds, some weighing as much as 22 pounds (10 kg) with wingspans up to 11 feet (3.5 m). With such long wings, these birds are masters of gliding over the water on strong air currents. All albatrosses have a stocky body build, webbed feet, and hooked beaks that help them snare prey. Like other seabirds, an albatross only comes to shore to mate and lay its egg, although young birds may spend the first two years of their lives inland. Before mating, birds carry out elaborate courtship rituals that include snapping the bills, flapping the wings, and aerial twists. A mated pair builds a volcano-shaped nest on which it lays only one egg.

Albatrosses do not have unusually small clutches by seabird standards. On the contrary, many seabirds produce only one or two eggs each breeding season. Scientists speculate that the reason for these small broods is the extreme distances that parents must fly to get food. The albatross, for example, feeds far from shore in the open sea. After producing an egg, each parent takes turns guarding the baby while the other travels hundreds of miles to feed. In addition to finding food for itself, a returning parent brings food for its new offspring. Unlike some species of birds, which return to their chicks with live prey held in their bills or talons, albatrosses swallow the food intended for their offspring, then regurgitate it on delivery. Two albatross parents, like the pair in the lower color insert on page C-7, stay busy supplying food for just one baby and would be unable to provide enough for a larger brood.

Most of the world's albatrosses live in the Southern Hemisphere. The largest species is the wandering albatross (*Diomedea exulans*), which ranges from Antarctica to the Tropics. It is a big animal that appears to be entirely white from a distance, but close inspection reveals that its plumage contains thin lines on the breast, neck, and upper back. The waved albatross (*Diomedea irrorata*) waddles when walking on the shore but is graceful in the sky. Taking flight from the beach can be a lot of work for such a large bird, so when possible, stepping off a sea cliff is a preferred method of getting in the air.

Fulmars resemble gulls but have heavier bills. The northern fulmar (*Fulmarus glacialis*) is the most common type in the northern latitudes. This bird has a gray neck, yellow bill, and dark wings that it holds out straight when gliding above the water.

Shearwaters, drab-colored birds with wingspans of about 45 inches (114.3 cm)., feed on krill and small fish plucked from the water's surface. Expert long-distance flyers, shearwaters nest on offshore islands around the world. The short-tailed shearwater (*Puffinus tenuirostris*) is sooty brown dorsally with pale ventral surfaces and wingspans over three feet (0.9 m).

The petrels are named for Saint Peter because, when reaching for prey with their feet, they seem to be walking on water. Found worldwide, petrels are the smallest representatives of the tube-nosed birds. Birds in this family, which includes both migratory and nonmigratory species, are dark brown or black with slender bills and long legs that seem too large proportionally for their bodies.

The flight patterns of storm petrels are erratic and fluttery, more like a moth than a typical bird. Wilson's storm petrel (*Oceanite oceanicus*) is a common species that hunts by flying low over the water's surface with its legs extended and feet peddling underwater in search of prey. Pairs of Wilson's storm petrels do not start breeding until they are four or five years old, quite late in life for such a small bird. Mating pairs return to the same nesting sight each year where they always lay one egg, migrating to their Antarctic breeding grounds from regions north of the equator in the Atlantic, Pacific, and Indian Oceans.

Diving petrels are tube-nosed birds with wingspans that are about 15 inches (38.1 cm) wide. Like other birds in the Procellariiformes family, diving petrels have stomach glands, hooked beaks, and tubenoses. Only found in the Southern Hemisphere, these birds physically resemble auks. Excellent vision helps diving petrel spot small fish from high in the air. Once a bird has a target, it dives headfirst into the water, continues the chase underwater by swimming, grabs its prey, and flies out of the water. The common diving petrel (*Pelecanoides urinatrix*), widespread around the southern oceans, has a brown back, mottled throat, and blue legs.

Auks and puffins, birds in the family Alcidae, are residents of the Northern Hemisphere that spend their winters at sea, congregating on land in the spring to lay their eggs. Like the albatrosses, a pair of auks lays only one egg each spring, and both parents spend all of their time keeping the chick supplied with food. Generally building their nests on the shores of small, rocky islands that have few predators, the birds breed around Iceland, Norway, the Faeroe Islands, British Isles, eastern Canada, and North America from Maine to the Canadian Arctic.

The strong, compact bodies and short, muscular wings of auks and other diving seabirds make them efficient and graceful underwater. On land, though, they are awkward and slow. Members of the auk family often have trouble getting airborne and may crash when they are trying to land.

The Atlantic puffin (*Fratercula arctica*) is one of four species of puffins that lives in the North Atlantic Ocean. During breeding season, the Atlantic puffin undergoes a dramatic change in plumage. In the winter, the bird's bill and plumage are dull-colored on the dorsal surface. However, in breeding season, the adult's bill widens and changes to bright orange, yellow, and blue and its feet turn orange. When breeding season is over, colors revert back to subdued tones.

At the age of four to five years, puffins mate, working as a pair to dig a nest on the ground with their bills and feet. One

Marine Bird Anatomy

Birds are warm-blooded vertebrates that have feathers to insulate and protect their bodies. In most species of birds, feathers are also important adaptations for flying. As a general rule, birds devote a lot of time and energy to keeping their feathers waterproof in a process called preening. During preening, birds rub their feet, feathers, and beaks with oil produced by the preen gland near their tail.

The strong, lightweight bones of birds are especially adapted for flying. Many of the bones are fused, resulting in the rigid type of skeleton needed for flight. Although birds are not very good at tasting or smelling, their senses of hearing and sight are exceptional. They maintain a constant, relatively high body temperature and a rapid rate of metabolism. To efficiently pump blood around their bodies, they have a four-chambered heart.

Like marine reptiles, marine birds have glands that remove excess salt from their bodies. Although the structure and purpose of the salt gland is the same in all marine birds, its location varies by species. In most marine birds, salt accumulates in a gland near the nostrils and then oozes out of the bird's body through the nasal openings.

The term *seabird* is not scientific but is used to describe a wide range of birds whose lifestyles are associated with the ocean. Some seabirds never get further out into the ocean than the surf water. Many seabirds are equipped with adaptations of their bills, legs, and feet. Short, tweezerlike bills can probe for animals that are near the surface of the sand or mud, while long, slender bills reach animals that burrow deeply. For wading on wet soil, many seabirds have lobed feet, while those who walk through mud or shallow water have long legs and feet with wide toes.

Other marine birds are proficient swimmers and divers who have special adaptations for spending time in water. These include wide bodies that have good underwater stability, thick layers of body fat for buoyancy, and dense plumage for warmth. In swimmers, the legs are usually located near the posterior end of the body to allow for easy maneuvers, and the feet have webs or lobes between the toes.

All marine birds must come to the shore to breed and lay their eggs. Breeding grounds vary from rocky ledges to sandy beaches. More than 90 percent of marine birds are colonial and require the social stimulation of other birds to complete the breeding process. Incubation of the eggs varies from one species to the next, but as a general rule the length of incubation correlates to the size of the egg: Large eggs take longer to hatch than small ones do.

large egg is deposited in the nest, and parents take turns incubating it. Once the hatchling gains some size, both parents leave it for short periods while they hunt for food.

Marine Mammals

Three types of mammals can be found living in deep, oceanic waters: pinnipeds, whales, and dolphins. Pinnipeds, the seals and their relatives, are mammals with finlike flippers. Whales, the largest mammals on Earth, display two distinctly different feeding styles and a variety of shapes and sizes. Dolphins are a small group of whalelike animals.

As a group, marine mammals are widespread and highly successful. Like seabirds, mammals divide each year into two distinct portions: breeding season and nonbreeding season. These two phases dictate where the animals are located, and the transition from one season to another is often marked by long migrations.

Social organization is strong among some types of marine mammals but less evident in others. Baleen whales have highly structured societies, and individuals remain in these groups their entire lives. Toothed whales are social animals but have less structure in their lives, often forming groups that are loose aggregates. Whales communicate with one another through sight and sound. Since sight is limited in the water, sound is the primary mode of exchanging information. Sounds vary by group and by species. The loudest sounds made by any animal are produced by the great whales.

At the surface of the water mammal behavior varies, with some species exhibiting acts like breaching, or jumping out of water, as well as tail and flipper slaps, while others surface only to get a breath of air. Whales will "spyhop," raise their heads above the water's surface, perhaps to look around. Many dolphins, pinnipeds, and whales are known to surf on waves, and some dolphins surf on the bow waves of ships.

Seals and their relatives are collectively known as pinnipeds, or the fin-footed animals. The streamlined body of a pinniped is fast and efficient in water, but slow and clumsy on land. To reduce drag while swimming, the animals are sleek, with very few protruding body parts; ears are either lacking or reduced, and genitals and teats are located inside the body. Another adaptation for swimming is flattened limbs, which act like broad fins. Many species are able to live in extremely cold environments because their bodies are protected by a thick layer of blubber located beneath the skin. In most species, pinniped males are much larger than females.

The pinnipeds are divided into two families, the Otariidae and Phocidae. Members of Phocidae lack external ear parts and are called the "true" seals. Phocidae cannot fold their hind limbs forward. When they move across the land they must hop on their bellies while supporting themselves with their front limbs, a mode of travel that has earned them the nickname "crawling seals." Those in the family Otariidae are known as the eared seals, a group that includes sea lions and fur seals. Otariidae have small external ears and hind limbs that can be folded forward to allow mobility on land. When out of water, the front flippers support the body, which can be walked forward on the hind limbs.

Northern fur seals (*Callorhinus ursinus*) are members of the Otariidae family. Adult males reach seven feet (2.1 m) in length and weigh up to 600 pounds (2.7 kg). Animals have small heads, short snouts, long hind flippers, and dark brown or black fur. Most of the year, northern fur seals swim alone in the northern Pacific Ocean, searching for food. In the spring, breeding colonies form on islands in the Bering Sea.

Like the individual in Figure 6.2 on page 108, northern fur seals are polygynous breeders, meaning that males establish territories into which they corral, and guard, females until mating season is over. A week after females come ashore in spring or early summer for mating, they give birth to the pup conceived the year before. Eight days after delivering, females are ready to mate again. New mothers stay ashore with their offspring, nursing them for three or four months. To feed, females leave their pups in nurseries that are guarded by members of the colony. When they return from foraging, females can find their own pups in the crowded nursery by sense of smell.

The largest pinnipeds in the Northern Hemisphere are the northern elephant seals (*Mirounga angustirostris*), members of

Fig. 6.2   Northern fur seals (Callorhinus ursinus) *come to shore in the spring to breed.*
(Courtesy of Captain Budd Christman, NOAA)

the family Phocidae. The adult male has an inflatable nose that hangs 10 inches (25 cm) over his lower lip when not inflated. Both males and females exhibit shades of brown, tan, or yellow. Males, which are four times larger than females, grow to 13.5 feet (4.1 m) in length and weigh up to 4,400 pounds (2,000 kg).

Eight to 10 months of the year, northern elephant seals swim in the Pacific Ocean. On dives as deep as 2,500 feet (800 m), the seals search for mesopelagic fish and squid. Seals make two annual trips to the coast: one for molting and the other for breeding. During molting, which may occur from late spring through summer, the animals spend much of their time sleeping on the beach, shedding large patches of skin and hair. In breeding season, from late January to early spring, males go ashore to assert their dominance with threats, vocal displays, and occasional fights. Winners earn the right to mate with females

Whales, or cetaceans, a group of more than 80 different species of animals, include the largest animals on Earth.

Cetaceans are streamlined marine mammals that are well adapted for life in the sea. Specialized feeding adaptations divide the animals into two major groups: baleen whales and toothed whales.

The mouths of baleen whales are equipped with strainers made of baleen, an elastic, hornlike material. Baleen plates enable the animals to strain zooplankton from the water. On their inside surfaces, the plates are covered with hair. The hair is smooth and silky in species that eat tiny zooplankton and thick and coarse in animals that eat small schooling fish. To feed, a baleen whale engulfs a large volume of water, then filters it through the baleen. Organisms that are trapped on the baleen plates are swallowed. Since baleen whales must strain a lot of water to satisfy their nutritional needs, their throats are pleated and expandable, enabling them to open their mouths extremely wide. Some baleen whales gulp water repeatedly during feeding, but others swim through the water with their mouths open. Figure 6.3 shows that baleen whales have two blowholes, making it possible for them to take in air

Fig. 6.3   Baleen whales have two blowholes and large mouths filled with baleen plates.

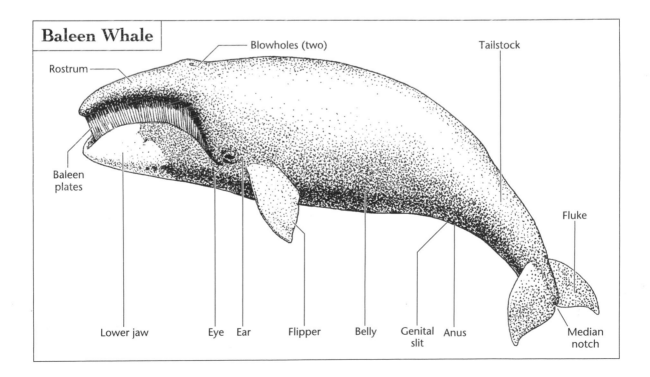

without completely surfacing. Oceanic baleen whales include the southern right, pygmy right, humpback, minke, dwarf minke, Antarctic minke, Bryde's, sei, fin, and blue whale.

Humpback whales (*Megaptera novaeangliae*) travel extensively and can be found in oceans all over the world. At the end of summer, humpbacks migrate from their warm-weather feeding grounds in the upper latitudes to mating and calving grounds in the tropics, a trip that involves more than 10,000 miles (16,000 km) of swimming. The behavior of humpback whales varies by season. During the summer, individuals form groups, communicating with behaviors such as breaching and slapping the water with fins or tails. In the winter, groups break apart and individuals do not feed, depending on the fat in their blubber to supply them with energy.

A humpback whale has flippers that are long, equal to one-third of its body length. Tubercles, round bumps that act as sensory organs, cover the head and lower jaw. Coloration is dark on the dorsal side and white or spotted on the ventral surface. The tail of a humpback is marked with notches that scientists can use to identify individuals. The tail of a humpback whale is shown in the upper color insert on page C-8.

Krill and small schooling fish supply the bulk of a humpback's food. Whales often feed alone but may work together to herd prey and make them easier to catch. Some whales use a bubble-net feeding technique, a method of blowing a wall of bubbles around a school of fish. The bubbles corral the fish into a narrow column, making it simple for the whale to swim through the school with its mouth wide open.

During breeding season, males sing songs that may function to attract females or send signals to other males to stay away. More than 20 males may compete for the attention of each female. Gestation lasts about a year, and females return to the Tropics to give birth to one calf.

The blue whale (*Balaenoptera musculus*) is the largest animal that has ever lived on Earth. An adult blue whale can reach lengths of 100 feet (30.5 m) and weigh as much as 400,000 pounds (180,000 kg). Females are usually larger than males. The skin of a blue whale is mottled and blue-gray in color. A small dorsal fin is set far back from the blowholes.

Blue whales are found in all of the world's major oceans. Females produce one calf every two to three years, traveling to the Tropics with the rest of their group to give birth. During the summers, the group migrates to the polar regions in search of food. Blue whales feed on krill, lunging into schools of the crustaceans to get big gulps. Each whale consumes about six tons (5,500 kg) of krill a day.

Toothed whales, a large group that includes sperm whales, dolphins, and porpoises, are carnivores that feed on fish, invertebrates, and other mammals. Only three species of sperm whales exist. Dolphins include Cuvier's beaked whale, northern and southern bottle-nosed whales, and the strap-toothed whale, as well as more familiar species such as the common bottle-nosed dolphin, spinner dolphins, and killer whales. One of the few species of porpoise that leads an oceanic lifestyle is Dall's porpoise.

The sperm whales (*Physeter macrocephalus*), known to many from Herman Melville's *Moby-Dick,* are named for the milky-white spermaceti in their heads, a material that early whalers mistook for sperm. Spermaceti is a liquid wax that is held in the spermaceti organ, located above and in front of the skull. The function of the organ is not known for certain, but it may be involved in either buoyancy or echolocation, the practice of emitting sound waves and listening for echoes to pinpoint objects in the environment.

Sperm whales are the largest toothed whales, and males, which are one-third larger than females, grow to 60 feet (18.3 m) long and weigh 120,000 pounds (57,000 kg). The main feature of a sperm whale is its large, rectangular head with its thin lower jaw. The blowhole is located toward the anterior end and set slightly to the left. The color is gray, and the dorsal fin is small, rounded, and set back on the body.

Although adult males can be found ranging in all parts of the ocean, populations of sperm whales favor canyons and continental slopes. Able to dive deeply and stay down a long time, the whales are efficient deepwater feeders. Some of their favorite prey includes bottom-dwelling fish, squid, octopuses, and rays. Females do not range as far as males, often forming long-term social groups of a dozen or so adults and their offspring. Males

Marine Mammal Anatomy

Mammals are warm-blooded vertebrates that have hair and breathe air. All females of this group have milk-producing mammary glands with which to feed their young. Mammals also have a diaphragm that pulls air into the lungs and a four-chambered heart for efficient circulation of blood. The teeth of mammals are specialized by size and shape for particular uses.

Marine mammals are subdivided into four categories: cetaceans, animals that spend their entire lives in the ocean; sirenians, herbivorous ocean mammals; pinnipeds, web-footed mammals; and marine otters. Animals in all four categories have the same characteristics as terrestrial mammals, as well as some special adaptations that enable them to survive in their watery environment.

The cetaceans, which include whales, dolphins, and porpoises, have streamlined bodies, horizontal tail flukes, and paddle-like flippers that enable them to move quickly through the water. Layers of blubber (subcutaneous fat) insulate their bodies and act as storage places for large quantities of energy. Their noses (blowholes) are located on the tops of their heads so air can be inhaled as soon as the organism surfaces above the water.

Manatees and dugongs are the only sirenians. These docile, slow-moving herbivores lack a dorsal fin or hind limbs but are equipped with front limbs that move at the elbow, as well as with a flattened tail. Their powerful tails propel them through the water, while the front limbs act as paddles for steering.

The pinnipeds—seals, sea lions, and walruses—are carnivores that have webbed feet. Although very awkward on land, the pinnipeds are agile and aggressive hunters in the water. This group of marine mammals is protected from the cold by hair and blubber. During deep-water dives, their bodies are able to restrict blood flow to vital organs and slow their heart rates to only a few beats a minute, strategies that reduce oxygen consumption. All pinnipeds come onto land or ice at breeding time.

The sea otters spend their entire lives at sea and only come ashore during storms. They are much smaller than the other marine mammals. Even though otters are very agile swimmers and divers, they are clumsy on shore. Their back feet, which are flipperlike and fully webbed, are larger than their front feet. Internally, their bodies are adapted to deal with the salt in seawater with enlarged kidneys that can eliminate the excess salt.

begin leaving the maternal group when they are about six years old. Mating occurs in the tropics during the spring.

Every four to six years, a female sperm whale produces one calf, which she nurses for two years.

The common bottle-nosed dolphin (*Tursiops truncates*) lives in temperate and tropical waters worldwide. Smaller than most other whales, male bottle-nosed dolphins grow to 12 feet (3.7 m) long and weigh up to 1,100 pounds (500 kg). Their color is gray, with much darker tones on the dorsal side than on the ventral. Very social animals, bottle-nosed dolphins form pods that are made up of related animals.

A well-known species of toothed whale is the killer whale, a large black-and-white marine mammal with a robust body, conical head, and tall dorsal fin, shown spy-hopping in the lower color insert on page C-8. A male killer whale may be 30 feet (9 m) long and weigh 12,000 pounds (5,600 kg). Although the species is cosmopolitan, the densest populations are in the high latitudes. Like many other whales, killer whales migrate, but scientists are not sure why. One hypothesis suggests that they simply follow their prey, which includes baleen whales, penguins, and seals.

Porpoises are marine mammals that resemble dolphins but are smaller and lack beaks. Dall's porpoise (*Phocoenoides dalli*), an oceanic species, usually occurs in small groups of two to 10 animals but can form large feeding aggregates of hundreds of animals. Distinctive black and white markings, a small head, round body, small flippers and triangular dorsal fin make Dall's porpoise relatively easy to identify. Males may be 7.3 feet (2.4 m) long and weigh 440 pounds (200 kg).

Dall's porpoise prefers the cool temperate waters of the North Pacific Ocean, especially along the continental slopes. These animals are very fast swimmers and hotly pursue small schooling fish and squid. Their primary predators are killer whales, but the porpoises are often able to outrun the slower whales.

Conclusion

Although more plentiful on land than in the sea, a substantial number of reptiles, birds, and mammals spend the majority of their lives in the open and deep oceans. As the descendants of terrestrial species, oceanic animals of all three groups have developed highly specialized adaptations for dealing with full-time, or almost full-time, life in the ocean.

The yellow-bellied sea snake is a highly venomous oceanic reptile. Yellow-bellied sea snakes attract fish by lying quietly on the sea's surface, imitating driftwood. When a fish swims over to relax in the shade of the snake, the lethal predator grabs it. If the fish makes a run for it, the snake can plunge under the water and pursue it for a short distance.

Three species of turtles in the open ocean include the green turtle, the loggerhead turtle, and the leatherback turtle. All are currently endangered as a result of exploitation in the previous century. All sea turtles spend the majority of their lives out at sea, coming ashore only to lay eggs. Turtles do not care for their offspring; once they have hatched young turtles are on their own as they scramble to the sea and try to avoid predators.

Birds that make their livings in the open sea include albatross, auk, booby, petrel, and shearwater. All seabirds spend the majority of their time at sea, returning to land to lay eggs and raise young. Because seabirds nest hundreds of miles from their feeding grounds, most mating pairs only raise one chick.

Mammals in the deep and open ocean include seals and their relatives, whales, and porpoises. Seals, members of a group called pinnipeds, have sleek bodies and flat, oarlike flippers. Northern fur seals and northern elephant seals are two species that spend the majority of their time away from the coast and shallow-water regions.

Most species of whales travel through the oceanic zones during seasonal migrations, and some species live there their entire lives. The baleen whales, those that filter small animals and zooplankton from the water, include the largest animal on Earth, the blue whale. Killer whales and bottle-nosed dolphins are among the toothed whales, a group of carnivorous animals. One small group of toothed whales, the sperm whales, have disproportionately long heads that contain a liquid wax whose exact function is still under debate.

7

The Mysterious Ocean

The part of the Earth that is habitable, the biosphere, is made up of the sea and the land. All of the Earth's terrestrial environments, including the soil, forests, rivers, fields, and plains, make up less than three percent of the biosphere. The rest of the habitable Earth is in the open and the deep ocean, a region that is largely unknown.

The largest proportion of the open ocean is deep water where life is sparse. The deep and open sea is dramatically different from the marine environments with which most people are familiar. Life abounds in ocean waters that are close to land, but at sea, populations are not as dense.

Harsh Environments

Far from the shore, low levels of nutrients restrict the growth of phytoplankton, even in the upper layers of water where there is plenty of light. The densities of diatoms and dinoflagellates drop away as the distance from land increases. In addition, the open sea is an inhospitable home for most marine plants. Except for sargassum weed, a brown alga that many animals cannot digest, seaweeds are nonexistent.

The number of living things in the deep sea decreases with depth. The only zone that receives enough light to carry out photosynthesis is the upper layer. Beneath the photic zone, organisms depend largely on foodfalls from above. Detritus drifting down through the water column is a critically important source of food and most is snatched up before it reaches the bottom. Only 20 percent makes it to the mesopelagic zone, and a mere five percent reaches the deep seafloor.

Not all of this detritus material is even edible. Some of the organic matter that drifts through the water column is made up of pellets of feces or other materials that cannot be consumed by animals that live in the water column. As a result, this matter cannot become part of the deep-sea food chain until it becomes food for bacteria. Animals are then able to feed on the bacterial colonies that grow on the detritus.

Deep seas are cold, dark, and under extremely high pressure. Animals have evolved some remarkable adaptations to survive these conditions. Since there is little light in the middle zones and no light on the seafloor, color is not an important characteristic, and most animals are colorless, black, or white. Many animals that live in the mesopelagic area either have enlarged eyes, or normal-sized eyes with heightened sensitivity. At great depths animals may lack eyes altogether.

In a world where there is so little food, predators have developed adaptations to make the most of any opportunity to catch food. Animals have large mouths, often making up half of their body length, and long, sharp teeth that point backward to prevent the escape of prey. Some deep-sea predators have evolved bioluminescent lures that help them attract prey.

Oxygen levels in much of the deep sea are low, and gills are enlarged to gather as much oxygen as possible. Some animals possess a very efficient form of hemoglobin that picks up more oxygen than the type found in shallow-water animals. In addition, deep-water animals are slow-moving, a behavioral adaptation that conserves energy and reduces the need for both food and oxygen. The muscle tissue of deepwater fish is flaccid and weak since swimming fast is not part of their lifestyle.

In a place where there are so few animals, it is very difficult to find a mate. Hermaphroditism helps solve that problem for many species. In some fish, the males parasitize females, attaching to them and remaining there throughout life. Other species have evolved special structures, such as bioluminescent glands, that generate mate-attracting light signals.

The Next Steps

Much of what is known about the deep sea has come from research conducted in a small, three-person submarine named *Alvin*. From the cramped seating inside of *Alvin*, deep-sea researchers have discovered hydrothermal vents and the collections of strange creatures that live around them. Dives to vents have also revealed the presence of chemosynthetic bacteria and the existence of food chains that are not dependent on energy from the Sun.

Only a fraction of the open and deep oceans have been explored. To understand this immense system, more research is needed. As marine scientists develop better ways to explore the seafloor, two schools of thought are emerging. There is a need to continue using and improving current technology. Ships, submersibles, and data from satellites are as important now as they were 30 years ago. To expand capabilities, a new deep-sea research vessel is being prepared to launch in 2008. An improvement over *Alvin* and similar subs, the new vessel will dive deeper, carry more people, and stay down longer. In addition, a new generation of remotely operated, unmanned, underwater vehicles (ROVs) are being developed.

The second approach is to establish a worldwide network of ocean observatories made up of moored buoys and telecommunications equipment. Each surface buoy would connect to a seafloor junction box that is wired with sensors. Data collected by the sensors would be transmitted to the buoy, and from there to a satellite. Such buoys could provide scientists all over the world with a wide range of data on weather, climate biology, and geology.

The deep sea is a new frontier, literally an unknown world, and a source of endless discoveries. Although most people will never visit the deep sea, research into the region may yield critically important resources for our future. Studies of the deep sea will also help scientists answer questions about the history of the Earth, including the changes in its environmental conditions. The Office of Ocean Exploration, established in 2000 by the National Oceanic and Atmospheric Administration (NOAA) based in Silver Spring, Maryland, supports ongoing research into all of those hard-to-get-to parts of the ocean. As technology evolves, humans have the opportunities to go where they have never been to before and to do things that were impossible to do in the past.

Glossary

A

algal bloom   The rapid growth of cyanobacteria or algae populations that results in large mats of organisms floating in the water.

amphibian   A cold-blooded, soft-skinned vertebrate whose eggs hatch into larvae that metamorphose into adults.

animal   An organism capable of voluntary movement that consumes food rather than manufacturing it from carbon compounds.

anterior   The region of the body that is related to the front or head end of an organism.

appendage   A structure that grows from the body of an organism, such as a leg or antenna.

arthropod   An invertebrate animal that has a segmented body, joined appendages, and chitinous exoskeleton.

asexual reproduction   A type of reproduction that employs means other than the union of an egg and sperm. Budding and binary fission are forms of asexual reproduction.

autotroph   An organism that can capture energy to manufacture its own food from raw materials.

B

binary fission   A type of cell division in monerans in which the parent cell separates into two identical daughter cells.

biodiversity   The number and variety of life-forms that exist in a given area.

bird   A warm-blooded vertebrate that is covered with feathers and reproduces by laying eggs.

bladder   In macroalgae, an inflatable structure that holds gases and helps keep blades of the plant afloat.

blade   The part of a nonvascular plant that is flattened and leaflike.

brood   A type of behavior that enables a parent to protect eggs or offspring as they develop.

budding   A type of asexual reproduction in which an offspring grows as a protrusion from the parent.

buoyancy   The upward force exerted by a fluid on matter that causes the matter to tend to float.

119

C

carnivore An animal that feeds on the flesh of other animals.

chanocyte A flagellated cell found in the gastrovascular cavity of a sponge that moves water move through the pores, into the gastrovascular cavity, and out the osculum (an exit for outflow).

chitin A tough, flexible material that forms the exoskeletons of arthropods and cell walls of fungi.

chlorophyll A green pigment, found in all photosynthetic organisms, that is able to capture the Sun's energy.

cilia A microscopic, hairlike cellular extension that can move rhythmically and may function in locomotion or in sweeping food particles toward an animal's mouth or oral opening.

cnidarian An invertebrate animal that is radially symmetrical and has a saclike internal body cavity and stinging cells.

cnidocyte A nematocyst-containing cell found in the tentacles of cnidarians that is used to immobilize prey or defend against predators.

countershading One type of protective, two-tone coloration in animals in which surfaces that are exposed to light are dark colored and those that are shaded are light colored.

cyanobacteria A moneran that contains chlorophyll as well as other accessory pigments and can carry out photosynthesis.

D

detritivore An organism that feeds on dead and decaying matter.

detritus Decaying organic matter that serves as a source of energy for detritivores.

DNA Deoxyribonucleic acid, a molecule located in the nucleus of a cell that carries the genetic information that is responsible for running that cell.

dorsal Situated on the back or upper side of an organism.

E

ecosystem A group of organisms and the environment in which they live.

endoskeleton An internal skeleton or support system such as the type found in vertebrates.

energy The ability to do work.

epidermis The outer, protective layer of cells on an organism, such as the skin.

exoskeleton In crustaceans, a hard but flexible outer covering that supports and protects the body.

F

fish   A cold-blooded, aquatic vertebrate that has fins, gills, and scales and reproduces by laying eggs that are externally fertilized.

flagellum   A long, whiplike cellular extension that is used for locomotion or to create currents of water within the body of an organism.

food chain   The path that nutrients and energy follow as they are transferred through an ecosystem.

food web   Several interrelated food chains in an ecosystem.

fungus   An immobile heterotrophic organism that consumes its food by first secreting digesting enzymes on it, then absorbing the digested food molecules through the cell walls of threadlike hyphae.

G

gastrodermis   The layer of cells that lines the digestive cavity of a sponge or cnidarian, and the site at which nutrient molecules are absorbed.

gastropod   A class of arthropods that has either one shell or no shells, a distinct head equipped with sensory organs, and a muscular foot.

gill   A structure containing thin, highly folded tissues that are rich in blood vessels and serve as the sites where gases are exchanged in aquatic organisms.

glucose   A simple sugar that serves as the primary fuel in the cells of most organisms. Glucose is the product of photosynthesis.

H

herbivore   An animal that feeds on plants.

hermaphrodite   An animal in which both male and female sexual organs are present.

heterotroph   An organism that cannot make its own food and must consume plant or animal matter to meet its body's energy needs.

holdfast   The rootlike portion of a macroalga that holds the plant to the substrate.

hydrogen bond   A weak bond between the positive end of one polar molecule and the negative end of another.

hyphae   Filamentous strands that make up the bodies of fungi and form the threadlike extensions that produce digestive enzymes and absorb dissolved organic matter.

I

invertebrate   An animal that lacks a backbone, such as a sponge, cnidarian, worm, mollusk, or arthropod.

L

lateral   The region of the body that is along the side of an organism.

lateral line   A line along the side of a fish that connects to pressure-sensitive nerves that enable the fish to detect vibrations in the water.

larva   The newly hatched offspring of an animal that is structurally different from the adult form.

light   A form of electromagnetic radiation that includes infrared, visible, ultraviolet, and X-ray that travels in waves at the speed of 186,281 miles (300,000 km) per second.

M

mammal   A warm-blooded vertebrate that produces living young that are fed with milk from the mother's mammary glands.

mantle   A thin tissue that lies over the organs of a gastropod and secretes the shell.

mesoglea   A jellylike layer that separates the two cell layers in the bodies of sponges and cnidarians.

milt   A fluid produced by male fish that contains sperm and is deposited over eggs laid by the female.

mixotroph   An organism that can use the Sun's energy to make its own food or can consume food.

molt   Periodic shedding of an outer layer of shell, feathers, or hair that allows new growth to occur.

moneran   A simple, one-celled organism that neither contains a nucleus nor membrane-bound cell structures.

motile   Capable of moving from place to place.

N

nematocyst   In cnidarians, a stinging organelle that contains a long filament attached to a barbed tip that can be used in defense or to capture prey.

O

omnivore   An animal that eats both plants and animals.

operculum   In fish, the external covering that protects the gills. In invertebrates, a flap of tissue that can be used to close the opening in a shell, keeping the animal moist and protecting it from predators.

oviparous   An animal that produces eggs that develop and hatch outside the mother's body.

ovoviviparous An animal that produces eggs that develop and hatch within the mother's body, then are extruded.

P

pectoral An anatomical feature, such as a fin, that is located on the chest.

pelvic An anatomical feature, such as a fin, that is located near the pelvis.

photosynthesis The process in which green plants use the energy of sunlight to make nutrients.

plant A nonmotile, multicellular organism that contains chlorophyll and is capable of making its own food.

polar molecule A molecule that has a negatively charged end and a positively charged end.

polychaete A member of a group of worms that has a segmented body and paired appendages.

posterior The region near the tail or hind end of an organism.

productivity The rate at which energy is used to convert carbon dioxide and other raw materials into glucose.

protist A one-celled organism that contains a nucleus and membrane-bound cell structures such as ribosomes for converting food to energy and Golgi apparati for packaging cell products.

R

radula A long muscle used for feeding that is covered with toothlike projections, found in most types of gastropods.

reptile A cold-blooded, egg-laying terrestrial vertebrate whose body is covered with scales.

S

salinity The amount of dissolved minerals in ocean water.

school A group of aquatic animals swimming together for protection or to locate food.

sessile Permanently attached to a substrate and therefore immobile.

setae Hairlike bristles that are located on the segments of polychaete worms.

sexual reproduction A type of reproduction in which egg and sperm combine to produce a zygote.

spawn The act of producing gametes, or offspring, in large numbers, often in bodies of water.

spicule   In sponges, a needle-like, calcified structure located in the body wall that provides support and protection.

spiracle   An opening for breathing, such as the blowhole in a whale or the opening on the head of a shark or ray.

stipe   A stemlike structure in a nonvascular plant.

surface tension   A measure of how easy or difficult it is for molecules of a liquid to stick together due to the attractive forces between them.

swim bladder   A gas-filled organ that helps a fish control its position in the water.

symbiosis   A long-term association between two different kinds of organisms that usually benefits both in some way.

T

territorial behavior   The defense of a certain area or territory by an animal for the purpose of protecting food, a mate, or offspring.

thallus   The body of a macroalgae, made up of the blade, stipe, and holdfast.

V

ventral   Situated on the stomach or lower side of an organism.

vertebrate   A member of a group of animals with backbones, including fish, amphibian, reptiles, birds, and mammals.

viviparous   An animal that gives birth to living offspring.

Z

zooxanthella   A one-celled organism that lives in the tissues of invertebrates such as coral, sponge, or anemone where it carries out photosynthesis.

Further Reading and Web Sites

Books

Banister, Keith, and Andrew Campbell. *The Encyclopedia of Aquatic Life*. New York: Facts On File, 1985. Well written and beautifully illustrated book on all aspects of the ocean and the organisms in it.

Coulombe, Deborah A. *The Seaside Naturalist*. New York: Fireside, 1990. A delightful book for young students who are beginning their study of ocean life.

Davis, Richard A. *Oceanography: An Introduction to the Marine Environment*. Dubuque, Iowa: Wm. C. Brown Publishers, 1991. A text that helps students become familiar with and appreciate the world's oceans.

Dean, Cornelia. *Against the Tide*. New York: Columbia University Press, 1999. An analysis of the impact of humans and nature on the ever-changing beaches.

Ellis, Richard. *Encyclopedia of the Sea*. New York: Alfred A. Knopf, 2000. A factual, yet entertaining, compendium of sea life and lore.

Garrison, Tom. *Oceanography*. New York: Wadsworth Publishing, 1996. An interdisciplinary examination of the ocean for beginning marine science students.

Karleskint, George, Jr. *Introduction to Marine Biology*. Belmont, Calif.: Brooks/ Cole-Thompson Learning, 1998. An enjoyable text on marine organisms and their relationships with one another and with their physical environments.

McCutcheon, Scott, and Bobbi McCutcheon. *The Facts On File Marine Science Handbook*. New York: Facts On File, 2003. An excellent resource that includes information on marine physical factors and living things as well as the people who have been important in ocean studies.

Nowak, Ronald M., et al. *Walker's Marine Mammals of the World*. Baltimore, Md.: Johns Hopkins University Press, 2003. An overview on the anatomy, taxonomy, and natural history of the marine mammals.

Pinet, Paul R. *Invitation to Oceanography*. Sudbury, Mass.: Jones and Bartlett Publishers, 2000. Includes explanations of the causes and effects of tides and currents, as well as the origins of ocean habitats.

Prager, Ellen J. *The Sea*. New York: McGraw-Hill, 2000. An evolutionary view of life in the Earth's oceans.

Reeves, Randall R., et al. *Guide to Marine Mammals of the World*. New York: Alfred A. Knopf, 2002. An encyclopedic work on sea mammals accompanied with gorgeous color plates.

Rice, Tony. *Deep Oceans*. Washington, D.C.: Smithsonian Museum Press, 2000. A visually stunning look at life in the deep ocean.

Sverdrup, Keith A., Alyn C. Duxbury, and Alison B. Duxbury. *An Introduction to the World's Oceans*. New York: McGraw Hill, 2003. A comprehensive text on all aspects of the physical ocean, including the seafloor and the ocean's physical properties.

Thomas, David. *Seaweeds*. Washington, D.C.: Smithsonian Museum Press, 2002. Illustrates and describes seaweeds from microscopic forms to giant kelps, explaining how they live, what they look like, and why humans value them.

Thorne-Miller, Boyce, and John G. Catena. *The Living Ocean*. Washington, D.C.: Friends of the Earth, 1991. A study of the loss of diversity in ocean habitats.

Waller, Geoffrey. *SeaLife: A Complete Guide to the Marine Environment*. Washington, D.C.: Smithsonian Institution Press, 1996. A text that describes the astonishing diversity of organisms in the sea.

Web Sites

Bird, Jonathon. *Adaptations for Survival in the Sea,* Oceanic Research Group, 1996. Available online. URL: http://www.oceanicresearch.org/adapspt.html. Accessed March 19, 2004. A summary and review of the educational film of the same name, which describes and illustrates some of the adaptations that animals have for life in salt water.

Buchheim, Jason. "A Quick Course in Ichthyology." Odyssey Expeditions. Available online. URL: http://www.marinebiology.org/fish.htm. Accessed January 4, 2004. A detailed explanation of fish physiology.

"Conservation: Why Care About Reefs?" REN Reef Education Network, Environment Australia. Available online. URL: http:www.reef.edu.au/asp_pages/search.asp. Accessed November 18, 2004. A superb Web site dedicated to the organisms living in and the health of the coral reefs.

Duffy, J. Emmett. "Underwater urbanites: Sponge-dwelling napping shrimps are the only known marine animals to live in colonies that resemble the societies of bees and wasps." *Natural History*. December 2003. Available online. URL: http://www.findarticles.com/cf_dls/m1134/10_111736243/print.jhtml. Accessed January 2, 2004. A readable and fascinating explanation of eusocial behavior in shrimp and other animals.

"Fungus Farming in a Snail." *Proceedings of the National Academy of Science,* 100, no. 26 (December 4, 2003). Available online. URL: http://www.pnas.org/cgi/content/abstract/100/26/15643. A well-written, in-depth analysis of the ways that snails encourage the growth of fungi for their own food.

Gulf of Maine Research Institute Web site. Available online. URL: http://www.gma.org/about_GMA/default.asp. Accessed January 2, 2004. A comprehensive and up-to-date research site on all forms of marine life.

"Habitat Guides: Beaches and Shorelines." eNature. Available online. URL: http://www.enature.com/habitats/show_sublifezone.asp?sublifezoneID=60# Anchor-habitat-49575. Accessed November 21, 2003. A Web site with young people in mind that provides comprehensive information on habitats, organisms, and physical ocean factors.

Huber, Brian T. "Climate Change Records from the Oceans: Fossil Foraminifera." Smithsonian National Museum of Natural History. June 1993. Available online. URL: http://www.nmnh.si.edu/paleo/marine/foraminifera.htm. Accessed December 30, 2003. A concise look at the natural history of foraminifera.

"Index of Factsheets." Defenders of Wildlife. Available online. URL: http://www.kidsplanet.org/factsheets. Accessed November 18, 2004. Various species of marine animals are described on this excellent Web site suitable for both children and young adults.

King County's Marine Waters Web site. Available online. URL: http://splash. metrokc.gov/wlr/waterres/marine/index.htm. Accessed December 2, 2003. A terrific Web site on all aspects of the ocean, emphasizing the organisms that live there.

Mapes, Jennifer. "U.N. Scientists Warn of Catastrophic Climate Changes." National Geographic News. February 6, 2001. Available online. URL: http://news.nationalgeographic.com/news/2001/02/0206_climate1.html. A first-rate overview of the current data and consequences of global warming.

National Oceanic and Atmospheric Administration Web site. Available online. URL: http://www.noaa.gov/. A top-notch resource for news, research, diagrams, and photographs relating to the oceans, coasts, weather, climate, and research.

"Resource Guide, Elementary and Middle School Resources: Physical Parameters." Consortium for Oceanographic Activities for Students and Teachers. Available online. URL: http://www.coast-nopp.org/toc.html. Accessed December 10, 2003. A Web site for students and teachers that includes information and activities.

"Sea Snakes in Australian Waters." CRC Reef Research Centre. Available online. URL: http://www.reef.crc.org.au/discover/plantsanimals/seasnakes. Accessed November 18, 2004. An overview of sea snake classification, breeding, and venom.

U.S. Fish and Wildlife Service Web site. Available online. URL: http://www.fws.gov/. A federal conservation organization that covers a wide range of topics, including fisheries, endangered animals, the condition of the oceans, and conservation news.

Index